COLOURS IN THE STORM

COLOURS IN THE STORM

JIM BETTS

Colours in the Storm
first published 2014 by
Scirocco Drama
An imprint of J. Gordon Shillingford Publishing Inc.

An earlier version was published by Playwrights Canada Press in 2000

Scirocco Drama Editor: Glenda MacFarlane
Cover design by Terry Gallagher/Doowah Design Inc.
Author photo by Richard Freedman
Printed and bound in Canada on 100% post-consumer recycled paper.

We acknowledge the financial support of the Manitoba Arts Council and The Canada Council for the Arts for our publishing program.

Production inquiries should be addressed to:
Catherine Knights, Catalyst TCM Inc.
#312-100 Broadview Avenue
Toronto, ON. M4M 3H3
416-645-0935 (ph)
416-645-0936 (fx)
catherine@catalysttcm.com
The printed music and recordings of the songs are also available through Catalyst.

Library and Archives Canada Cataloguing in Publication

Betts, Jim, author
Colours in the storm / Jim Betts.

A play.
Previously published: Toronto : Playwrights Canada Press
, 2000, ©1990.
ISBN 978-1-927922-06-4 (pbk.)

1. Thomson, Tom, 1877-1917--Drama. I. Title.

PS8553.E853C64 2014 C812'.54 C2014-907530-8

J. Gordon Shillingford Publishing
P.O. Box 86, RPO Corydon Avenue, Winnipeg, MB Canada R3M 3S3

Acknowledgements

The Ontario Arts Council, The Canada Council for the Arts, The Laidlaw Foundation, Victoria Steele, Young People's Theatre, Doug Ellis, CAMTA, Factory Lab, Muskoka Festival, Tapestry Music Theatre, and Theatre Organgeville.

Developing artists for the first production were: Michael Ayoub, Suzanne Bennett, Elise Dewsberry, Melanie Doane, Judith Farthing, Rachel Glover, Shelley Hanson, Ed Henderson, Kate Hennig, Lee MacDougall, Shane McPherson, David Nairn, Barry Peters, Ralph Small, Marcia Tratt, Judy Uwiera, Jonathan Whittaker, Stephen Woodjetts and Patrick Young.

Production History

The original production of *Colours in the Storm* was a co-production between the Muskoka Festival and Arbour Theatre Company, Peterborough in 1990, with following the creative team:

Tom Thomson .... Jonathan Whittaker

Mark Robinson, Martin Bletcher, et al........ Ralph Small

Winnie Trainor .... Suzanne Bennett

Shannon Fraser, Larry Dixon, et al .... Shane McPherson

Annie Fraser, Frances McGillvray, et al .... Elise Dewsberry

Pianist .... Stephen Woodjetts

Guitarist........ Mike Allen

Fiddler/Mandolin........ Shelley Coopersmith

Directed by Michael Ayoub

Musical Direction and Vocal Arrangements by Stephen Woodjetts

Orchestration and Arrangements by Ed Henderson

Set and Lighting Design by Rod Hillier

Costume Design by David Juby

Choreography by Caroline Smith

Stage Manager: Madelyne Keane

Assistant Stage Manager: Theresa Malek

Apprentice Stage Manager: Judith Begley

Colours in the Storm was produced by Theatre Aquarius in 1998 with the following creative team:

Tom Thomson .... Jonathan Whittaker

Winnie Trainor .... Suzanne Bennett

Mark Robinson, Martin Bletcher, et al.............................Ralph Small

Shannon Fraser, Lawren Harris, et all..................... Lee MacDougall

Larry Dixon, Hugh Trainor, et al........................... Shane McPherson

Wild Mary, Annie Fraser, et al ....Naomi Emmerson

Marie Trainor, Frances McGillvray, et al........................Sheila Brand

James MacCallum et al .... Brian Rhodes

Pianist ....Charles Cozens

Guitarist... Mike Allen

Fiddler/Mandolin... Shelley Coopersmith

Directed by Jim Betts

Musical Direction by Charles Cozens

Set and Costume Design by Jonathan Porter

Lighting Design by Louise Guinand

Sound Design by Mike Stewart

Choreography by Max Reimer

Stage Manager: Stephen Newman

Assistant Stage Manager: Cindy Jenningsa

Cast of Characters

TOM THOMSON:...................... Passionate, mercurial, and increasingly possessed by his artistic vision; 35 years old in 1912

WINNIE TRAINOR:................. Confident, capable and Thomson's equal in most things; a few years younger than Thomson

MARTIN BLETCHER:.............. Quiet, emotionally repressed, but capable of anger; considers himself Thomson's rival for Winnie

SHANNON FRASER:............... "The big Irishman"; powerful and quick to anger; jealous of and increasingly aggravated by Thomson

ANNIE FRASER:........................ Hard-working and good-hearted; endlessly intrigued by Thomson; comes to understand her own strengths

LARRY DIXON:.......................... Poacher, guide and self-proclaimed "expert woodsman"; makes a mean vat of hooch

MARK ROBINSON:.................. Park ranger, diarist; grows to become one of Thomson's few friends

WILD MARY:............................. An uncontrolled spirit of the bush, alert to and embracing of the dangers and passions of the park

FRANCES McGILLVRAY:........ An artist; self-confident, intelligent, goes after what she wants; in her 50s

MARIE TRAINOR: .... Determined to be a proper mother, she has somehow sublimated a real strength and determination

HUGH TRAINOR:.................... Runs the local lumber yard, tolerates his wife's desire to be sociable and genteel

DR JAMES MacCALLUM:....... Ophthalmologist, art patron, businessmen; wry and intelligent; becomes Thomson's patron, agent and friend

LAWREN HARRIS:................... A founder of The Group of Seven; spiritual; well-spoken

ALICE LAMBERT: .... 15, vivacious, unaffected, determined

Jim Betts

Jim Betts is a fixture in Canadian musical theatre, and is an award-winning writer and composer. His productions *Colours in the Storm, Little Women, The Shooting of Dan McGrew, Jacob Two-Two Meets the Hooded Fang* and *The Mystery of the Oak Island Treasure* have been performed in theatres across Canada. He is currently the Artistic Director of Smile Theatre, a unique company that creates and presents high-quality performances by outstanding theatre artists to seniors who are isolated from cultural experiences. For more information about Jim's plays and musicals. please go to www.jimbetts.ca.

Scene/Song Breakdown

A Note on this Version of *Colours in the Storm*

Colours in the Storm has undergone a lengthy development. It was originally commissioned and workshopped by Michael Ayoub and The Muskoka Festival in the late 1980s, and first reached the stage in 1990 as a co-production between the Muskoka Festival and Arbour Theatre Company in Peterborough. That 1990 production was revived, with a number of script changes, in 1991.

A few years later, Tapestry Music Theatre sponsored a re-examination of the script, and a new draft was developed with Urjo Kareda as dramaturge. Under the direction of Martha Henry, that script was then workshopped by Tapestry and subsequently produced as part of a seven-week tour through Ontario in 1994. That tour featured seven actors and four musicians. The show was then adapted the following year into a one-act format and toured by Tapestry through the schools in association with Prologue to The Performing Arts.

Yet another revised script was produced by Theatre Orangeville in 1997, and that script revised yet again for Theatre Aquarius in the fall of 1998. It is that Theatre Aquarius version of the show—performed by a cast of eight actors and three musicians—that is represented here.

The show as currently written could be performed by as many as twelve (or more) actors, and by many more musicians. That production, however, has yet to happen.

For Theatre Aquarius, all of the actors except Jonathan Whittaker (as Thomson) doubled at least once. Those doubles were: Bletcher/Robinson, Fraser/Harris, Marie/Frances, Wild Mary/Annie and Dixon/Hugh; all of those combinations, as well as the actors playing Winnie and MacCallum, also doubled as "Shades". It is possible to change how the doubling works, and in fact no two productions have used the same doubling breakdowns.

Because the story moves quickly through many different locations, the set needs to be as flexible as possible. Jonathan Porter's set for the Theatre Aquarius production was beautifully evocative of Algonquin Park: it featured three main acting areas defined by riser units, each of a different size and shape; there was then a beautiful backdrop based on one of Thomson's sky paintings balanced by a number of translucent screens to either side based on motifs from Thomson's "Northern River" painting.

Props and costumes were realistic (although early productions of the show used as few real props as possible). Jonathan Whittaker as Thomson actually painted onstage as part of the show (and the pre-show), so many of the "boards" and paints were real working props. Other "boards" were facsimiles of some of Thomson's relevant paintings.

Two very specific design/performance choices were made in this production, as they were in 1990 in Muskoka.

A rain barrel was a prominent part of the set, where "Larry Dixon" often stood and accompanied scenes. Shane McPherson played Dixon (and "Algonquin Park") in the original Muskoka production, and again in 1997-98 at Theatre Orangeville and Theatre Aquarius. Standing by the barrel, and with the use of a few props or whistled bird and loon calls, Shane managed to create a wonderful soundscape and almost musical underscore to certain scenes. He would create the sounds of Canoe Lake, or a river or a canoe trip by using a canoe paddle to stir the water in the barrel. He had a set of "spoons" that he used to make the sound of skipping stones in Scene 6, or to accompany "The One That Got Away." He had small stones (of various sizes) tied to strings that he used for the sound of fishing lures hitting the water in Scene 12, or Bletcher's "plop" in Scene 6. And he had a watering can that he used while Thomson was standing in the canoe in Scene 12. More than any other single choice, I think the use of the rain barrel is what gave those particular productions their unique sense of style.

Every production of *Colours in the Storm* will eventually have to decide how to deal with the canoe scenes. The Tapestry Music Theatre production, designed by Jim Plaxton, used a wonderfully alive canoe based on a kind of "swiveling teeter-totter" design. The choice we made was far simpler. The original Muskoka Theatre production used a stationery bench—all the actual movement of the canoe in the water was created by the actors. In the 1997-98 Orangeville and Aquarius productions, we made three separate canoe choices: in "Thunderhead" Thomson used the edge of the stage as his canoe;

in "The One That Got Away" and "Still Water/White Water" we used a wooden bench; and in the more surrealistic "Just A Little Farther" scene in Act II, Thomson and Robinson stood in separate isolated specials and "paddled" standing up, shifting their bodies in unison as the canoe went in new directions.

The stage directions included in this script are meant to give the reader a feeling of how the Theatre Aquarius production worked. It is possible, however, to interpret the story in any number of physical settings and by using as much imagination as possible in how the show is staged.

One of the main themes of the show is the search for artistic perfection. That is never going to happen, and it certainly hasn't yet been achieved by *Colours in the Storm*. But we can keep trying, and so I encourage anyone who produces the show in the future to continue that search.

Jim Betts

Act I

Part One—Pinewood Arms To Hold Me

Scene 1—Where Once We've Felt The Colours

Colours and sounds of Spring in Algonquin Park—water, leaves, wildlife. THOMSON is discovered at his campsite, painting. The light changes. Sounds ebb and flow. Eventually there is darkness, then music.

WILD MARY appears.

"Algonquin"

WILD MARY: Here in the hush
Stand the gods of Algonquin,
Here stand the spruce
And the wind-swept pine.
Here in the mist
Hidden deep in Algonquin
Spirit enchants
This Algonquin shrine.

More figures appear out of the shadows.

Here in the Spring
Cracks the ice of Algonquin.
White water stirs
As the west winds sting.
Colours are buds
On the leaves of Algonquin
Bursting like flame
To Algonquin Spring.

Where the water is cold
And the wind is uncontrolled
Where the flesh is weak
But the current's always strong.
In Algonquin.

COMPANY: Algonquin.

THOMSON moves through the FIGURES and the trees.

Wild runs the blood
Through the heart of Algonquin,
Dark is the night
As the ravens cry.
Anger glows red
In the eyes of Algonquin
Danger waits under
Algonquin sky.

WILD MARY: Where the storms bend the trees,

COMPANY: And may drive us to our knees

THOMSON: But where once we've felt the colours
We belong

COMPANY: To Algonquin.
Algonquin.
Algonquin.

MARK ROBINSON steps forward.

Scene 2—The Ghost Story

MARK ROBINSON consults a small diary. DIXON moves in to listen, and to comment. The rest of the COMPANY gathers behind them. WILD MARY observes, unseen. THOMSON watches from a distance.

ROBINSON: Monday July 16th, 1917—the body of a man is

discovered in the waters of Canoe Lake, Algonquin Park. Reports indicate there is fishing line wrapped sixteen or seventeen times around one ankle, some evidence of bleeding from one ear, and a four-inch bruise across the left temple. The coroner concludes "Accidental death by drowning."

DIXON: Without ever botherin' to look at the body.

ROBINSON: The first report of the man's disappearance had been seven days earlier, July 9th, his overturned canoe having been found floating on the lake. The day after the canoe was found…

DIXON: …for some reason no one's ever rightly explained to me…

ROBINSON: …the canoe disappeared again.

More figures step into the light.

Fifteen years later, a painter from the Group of Seven, a Mr. Lawren Harris, came to visit a family in the Park.

LAWREN HARRIS: It was August. I had accepted an invitation to a day of fishing. And it was approaching dusk as we began canoeing home.

VOICE 1 : A mist was rising from the water.

HARRIS: When suddenly the youngest daughter shouted:

VOICE 2: "Look! Father must be coming to meet us."

HARRIS: I turned towards the moon to see where the child was pointing and there, kneeling in a canoe and paddling towards us, was a man—now a little less than a hundred yards away.

A loon calls.

HARRIS: A loon cried from the other side of the lake and the little girl jumped.

VOICE 2: I was getting frightened but I didn't know why.

HARRIS: But then the man in the canoe lifted his arm and waved at us.

VOICE 2: And suddenly I felt better.

HARRIS: And just as he was almost close enough for us to see his face, a cloud covered the moon.

A second loon call.

And when the moon reappeared, he was gone.

VOICE 2: The man, the canoe—everything.

HARRIS: He was simply no longer there.

ROBINSON: The child kept insisting later that the man was wearing a yellow shirt.

VOICE 1 : Father never wears yellow, dear.

ROBINSON: The man they described having seen that night was the same man whose body was discovered in that water fifteen years earlier—painter and outdoorsman, Tom Thomson.

DIXON: Ranger Robinson told 'em later they had to have been seeing things.

ROBINSON: Mr. Harris, being a more spiritual man than some…

HARRIS: It is a popular belief that I have no intention of disputing that those who depart before their time continue to haunt the lands they loved. I am certain that what we saw that night was the spirit of Tom Thomson.

DIXON: For years afterward folkso 'round the park used to argue about what colour shirt Thomson had been wearing when he drowned.

VOICE 2: I like to think it was yellow.

VOICE 3: I think it was yellow.

WILD MARY: It was yellow.

HARRIS: After Thomson's death in 1917, the park wardens and guides searched every inch of Canoe Lake for Tom's hand-painted canoe and paddle.

ROBINSON: They were never found.

THOMSON steps forward.

Scene 3—The Frozen Waterfall

THOMSON: I'd never seen a frozen waterfall until I saw one in Algonquin Park. It's an unnerving sight. There it is, this immense cacophony of ice—but when it glistens in the winter sun a little surface water scurries into these tiny rivers. Or more precisely into the illusion of rivers, because the real power is still hidden somewhere deep inside. Dig a hole and put your hand in to find that power and the frost would bite it off. That waterfall on a windless night makes no sound at all, frozen so solid bullets would bounce off. But in the Spring…in the Spring it has the power to inspire, and destroy.

WINNIE, WILD MARY and FRANCES move to THOMSON.

Scene 4—An Ordinary Man

"The Girl With Thunder In Her Hair"

WOMEN: In the Spring the ice cracks like thunder,
And the wind moves the branches
Like a woman's hair,
And the colours in the wildflowers
Flash like a woman's eyes,

And the pine boughs reach for us like lovers.

THOMSON: I was on the road
One windless April day
When I could hear a rumbling
In the trees not far away.
I turned around
To face the sound
And she was standing there—
A girl with thunder in her hair.

VOICES gradually join THOMSON.

She held out her hand
And with a voice so green, said:

THOMSON
& WOMEN: "Come and let me show you things
No man has ever seen."

THOMSON: But I said no
I shall not go
But then to my surprise
I could see the lightning in her eyes.

THOMSON
& WOMEN: "Come away with me
And together we will be

THOMSON: Two stormy west wind lovers
In a tumble o'er the sea.

THOMSON
& WOMEN: Come and touch my dress
Feel the rain in my caress."

THOMSON: I was tempted, yes, but did I dare

THOMSON
& MEN: Go with the girl with thunder in her hair?

WOMEN: (Pine boughs reach for us like lovers.)

THOMSON: As an ordinary man
There are rules I mustn't break.
Roads I mustn't travel
And risks I daren't take.

THOMSON
& MEN: And yet when she
Appeared to me I couldn't help but care
For the girl with thunder in her hair.

THOMSON
& WOMEN: "Come away with me
And together we will be

THOMSON: Like leaves upon a river
In a tumble to the sea

THOMSON
& WOMEN: Come and touch my skin
Like a lover's mandolin

THOMSON: Take the river in beneath the changing skies."

ALL: Said the girl with lightning in her eyes.

THOMSON: But I dared not go
With so much I didn't know
So I turned back towards the city
And the wind began to blow.
But her eyes flashed gold
And her hair flew uncontrolled
Till I couldn't bear not being there

ALL: With the girl with thunder in her hair.

All but WINNIE exit.

Scene 5 —The Witch Of Huntsville

WINNIE: I know what they're saying. The children call me a witch. To their parents, of course, I'm just —"Wild Winnie"—that crazy old spinster who lost her last chance at a man in the waters of Canoe Lake. But to the writers, the busybodies, the "journalists", it's: "Is it true you were engaged to him, Miss Trainor?" "Is it true that when he died you were pregnant with his child?" "Care to comment, old woman, on the rumours that he committed suicide rather than marry you?" "Tell us, Miss Trainor—who really killed Tom Thomson?" I'm seventy-seven this year. And tonight, forty years ago, he disappeared never to be found alive again. They say I changed after he died. That I've kept too many things buried inside myself. When what they really mean is, they so desperately want to know what I know.

WINNIE crosses to DIXON's barrel, where he hands her a fishing pole.

Well, this much I will tell you: I was fishing when we met. And I was always damn better at fishing than he ever was.

WINNIE crosses to the shore of Canoe Lake and casts her line into the water.

Part Two—Standing In The Shadows

Scene 6—Skipping Stones

Shore of Canoe Lake, 1912. WINNIE is fishing from shore. MARTIN BLETCHER appears behind her.

BLETCHER: Any luck, Winnie?

WINNIE: No need for luck, Martin. Fishing is an art.

BLETCHER: Haven't caught anything then.

WINNIE: Not a nibble.

WINNIE hands her fishing rod to BLETCHER and skips a stone. BLETCHER tries to work up some nerve.

BLETCHER: Bessie's invited Harry McLeod to our place for supper tonight.

WINNIE: Your sister and Harry McLeod?

WINNIE skips another stone; she's very good at it.

BLETCHER: I wondered if you'd like to come, too.

WINNIE: I'm making dinner for my folks tonight.

BLETCHER: Sure. *(Hands the rod to WINNIE, then tries to skip a stone, it goes plop.)* Some other time, maybe.

WINNIE: *(Something catches her interest out on the lake.)* Who's that?

BLETCHER: *(Also looking onto the lake.)* I don't know. But whoever it is can't paddle a canoe. Look at that—he can hardly keep it on the water.

WINNIE: He's not that bad, Martin.

BLETCHER: Must be from the city. Oh, look at that—he's terrible! Probably from Toronto.

WINNIE: He's coming ashore here. Now keep your voice down.

BLETCHER: Doesn't even know how to get out of it.

Enter THOMSON with some painting paraphernalia.

THOMSON: ...Hello.

BLETCHER: First time in a canoe, friend?

THOMSON: I'm a little out of practice.

BLETCHER: I hope you can swim.

WINNIE: That doesn't look like fishing gear.

THOMSON: No. For a less demanding art, I'm afraid.

WINNIE: You see, Martin—fishing *is* an art.

BLETCHER: …I fish.

THOMSON: I'd enjoy chasing a few trout—if I knew where to cast.

WINNIE: If you stay awhile I could take you out and show you. Ours is the first white cabin past the point.

BLETCHER: And ours is the big one two down.

WINNIE: You're staying at the Mowat Lodge?

THOMSON: I will be. I'm just up from the city today. I could've gone with the wagon they sent to the station, but I wanted to see all this from the water first. Silly, I suppose. Because I really have no idea at the moment where the Mowat Lodge is.

BLETCHER points helpfully toward the Mowat.

WINNIE: You're the painter, I expect. …You're not going to cut off your ear, I hope?

BLETCHER: What?

THOMSON: Only if it will make effective bait.

BLETCHER: What are you two on about?

WINNIE: My father and I are going out tomorrow about five. If you'd care to angle with us…

THOMSON: First white cabin past the point.

BLETCHER: I might do some fishing tomorrow myself.

WINNIE: If you get lost ask for the Trainors.

THOMSON: Until tomorrow morning then, Miss Trainor.

THOMSON exits.

BLETCHER: *(Calling after Thomson, identifying himself.)* …Martin Bletcher. …You don't even know his name.

WINNIE: Of course I do. His name's Tom Thomson. Care to walk me home, Martin?

BLETCHER is a little confused, but exits after WINNIE.

Scene 7—It Matters More Now

Veranda of Mowat Lodge. THOMSON sets up his paints and begins to sketch. SHANNON FRASER talks to the audience.

SHANNON: *(With a bit of an Irish lilt.)* The name's Shannon Fraser. For seventeen years I ran the Mowat Lodge: two miles from the train depot, and even closer to the Canoe Lake burying-ground. Location is everything. Thirteen years after Thomson died, the Mowat burnt to the ground and I left this park forever. But, as they say, the legend of Shannon Fraser stayed on. It was me reported having seen Thomson canoe off that last morning—last man to see him alive. But it was also me got accused, by my own wife no less—o' havin' murdered Thomson myself. Tried to sell his boots after his death, I did, if you believe them that says it. Though if truth be told, check out the picture he done o' me if you don't think he looked at me with as much red in his eyes as I had lookin' at him. Anyway, this is the Mowat Lodge. It weren't such a bad place in those days. Food was edible, no mosquitoes in the whiskey. And it's where the great Tom Thomson used to stay till the snow went. Snow never went soon enough for me.

ANNIE pushes MacCALLUM onto the veranda in a wheelchair.

ANNIE: Here you go, Doctor. Into our good Algonquin Park air.

MacCALLUM: Thank you, Mrs Fraser.

ANNIE: And I brung a blanket. Against the chill.

SHANNON: A bit of hooch, perhaps, Doctor? For the parts of a man no blanket can warm.

ANNIE: It's rest the Doctor needs, Shannon—and fresh air.

MacCALLUM: I don't want to be a bother. *(Looking at THOMSON.)* And if this gentleman is going to find me a nuisance, I can just as easily…

ANNIE: Doctor, please—I'd rather hoped you and Tom might…

SHANNON: Annie.

ANNIE stops immediately.

I don't see the Doctor's breakfast tray.

ANNIE exits.

Stay right where you are, Doctor, and meet a fellow guest. Dr. MacCallum—Tom Thomson.

THOMSON: Doctor.

MacCALLUM: It's Jim.

SHANNON: Just in on yesterday's train. Here for the cure.

THOMSON: If I'm going to disturb you… *(Moves to leave.)*

SHANNON: Good of you to go, Thomson.

THOMSON: It's just that the light here…

MacCALLUM: Please—for the next few months I'm to be considered part of the flora and fauna.

THOMSON: ...Thank you.

MacCALLUM: You're a painter, Tom.

THOMSON: No.

MacCALLUM: I've met a few painters; though not many modest ones. In fact, it was Lawren Harris who recommended this Lodge. Said there's something about the colours up here. Which is true, I suppose—if you like green. You know Lawren?

THOMSON: I know he's a fine painter.

MacCALLUM: ...Have you some I can see?

THOMSON considers a moment, then pulls a few boards out of his kit and hands them to MacCALLUM. ANNIE re-enters with a tray, and looks over MacCALLUM's shoulder.

ANNIE: Are these all yours, Tom?

MacCALLUM and ANNIE look at the paintings intently, making THOMSON uncomfortable. They look at the paintings, then at THOMSON, as if posing to themselves perceptive, humiliating but unasked questions. MacCALLUM registers a certain puzzlement.

MacCALLUM: ...They're good, aren't they?

THOMSON: Well—they're just—sketches.

ANNIE: I think they're very good.

SHANNON: Hot Mush!

ANNIE: Shannon!

SHANNON: No offense, Thomson, but ain't that more like a gargle, or a gob of porridge, than an honest paintin'?

MacCALLUM: No offense taken, I'm sure. ...You've studied, Tom?

THOMSON: A lesson or two.

MacCALLUM examines one in particular.

MacCALLUM: You actually saw these colours in this park?

THOMSON: Yes. *(Points a spot nearby.)* There. ...Last Thursday. ...Seven AM.

ANNIE finally spots a painting she does in fact like.

ANNIE: ...I used to wish I could do this. Pictures. Where my mother worked, I used to look at the drawings in the books they had. Wondering what the stories were. Wanting to go to those places. Maybe do my own pictures of the things I'd see.

THOMSON: And did you?

ANNIE: No.

THOMSON: Then you should now.

ANNIE: No.

THOMSON takes back the boards, then impulsively gives each of them the one painting they liked.

THOMSON: Please.

ANNIE: I couldn't.

MacCALLUM: Tom, I didn't mean...

THOMSON: It's not a Lawren Harris, Doctor, but...

MacCALLUM: It's Jim. And I accept. *(Takes the sketch.)*

ANNIE: ...Thank you. *(Takes the sketch.)*

THOMSON: I'm no expert, Mrs. Fraser—but I could teach you what little I know about this.

SHANNON: She's not interested, Thomson.

THOMSON: At least help you get started.

MacCALLUM: It's a generous offer.

ANNIE: That was a long time ago. It don't matter now.

THOMSON: It matters more now.

SHANNON: Enough to be done 'round here without taking time for foolishness.

SHANNON takes the painting from ANNIE and gives it back to THOMSON.

THOMSON: Well, the offer's made.

SHANNON: ...We'd best be getting to our chores, Annie.

MacCALLUM: You don't mind if we keep her a few more minutes, do you, Fraser? ...I'll need someone to take away my tray.

SHANNON: ...To *my* chores then.

SHANNON exits. THOMSON resumes painting.

MacCALLUM: Now we mustn't bother Tom any more this morning, Mrs Fraser. Genius at work. Vanguard of the new Hot Mush School of Canadian Art. As for you, Tom, you've a way to go yet to convince me about those colours. Though perhaps if you painted it warmer, it would *be* warmer. Or better yet, take pity on an old man and paint me in the south of France, on a sun-swept beach—without a spot on my lung.

THOMSON: *(His attention still elsewhere.)* I'll do that, Doctor.

ANNIE retrieves the painting SHANNON gave back to THOMSON.

MacCALLUM: Lovely. It feels warmer already.

MacCALLUM closes his eyes to nap. ANNIE watches THOMSON.

Scene 8—Over The Dam

Outside the Trainor cottage.

"Over The Dam"

WINNIE: I remember the treehouse
My father built down by the dam
Where I'd sit by the hour with books
And mom's biscuits and jam.
Now the treehouse is gone
Though the river runs on
And the water slips over the dam.
As the girl that I was
Slips away from the woman I am.

There's a bay where the water
Was warm as a night in July,
Where we called out like loons
And we prayed one day one might reply
Now it's too cold to swim
And we're all much too prim
To exclaim like a bird to the sky.
Like the girl calling out
To the woman who can't hear her cry.

Yes, the water gets colder
Like friendships as they get older
And the water where children swam
Goes over the dam.

There's a shine on the water
And colours that I've never seen.
And the sheen on the pine
I remember as never this green.
There's a feeling today

I can't let get away
So I'll climb in my childhood canoe
And when all this goes over the dam
This time I'm going, too.

WINNIE moves to her garden.

Scene 9—Planting The Garden

WINNIE begins working on the garden. A storm is closing in. MARIE enters from the Trainor cabin. THOMSON enters from the trees. THOMSON appears energized and restless—distracted by the coming storm.

MARIE TRAINOR: Winnifred, darling. Surely you're not going to do that now?

WINNIE: It's almost finished. If I can get it done before the storm hits, the rain will get it off to a good start.

MARIE: But you have a guest.

WINNIE: Oh—Mr. Thomson. I was hoping he might help.

MARIE: Mr. Thomson, I do apologize for my daughter.

THOMSON: It's the least I can do, in return for the invitation.

MARIE: Oh, it's been no trouble. A simple, humble pot roast.

WINNIE: I'm sure it will seem like a feast, Mother, Mr. Thomson being more used to pancakes and bacon, I think. And what few fish he can catch.

THOMSON: I'm catching more.

HUGH TRAINOR enters.

HUGH TRAINOR: Why are we coming out here? It's going to rain, for god's sake.

MARIE: Hugh, your language.

HUGH: What's the matter with my goddamn language? How 'bout a brandy, Thomson?

THOMSON: ...Yes—thank you.

HUGH: Good lad. Excuse for me to have one.

WINNIE: I'll join you, father.

MARIE: Winnifred!

HUGH exits for the brandy.

WINNIE: Please don't fuss, mother. You'll give Mr Thomson entirely the wrong idea about us. She hardly fusses at all, Mr. Thomson. She's really just as bohemian as the rest of us.

MARIE: I most certainly am not!

WINNIE: *(To THOMSON.)* Could you clear a patch over there?

MARIE: Over there? We never have a part of the garden over there.

WINNIE: For the carrots.

MARIE: The carrots? The carrots go over there. They've gone over there for ten years. What are you going to put over there?

WINNIE: I thought, peas.

MARIE: The peas go over there! Winnie Trainor, what in the world has gotten into you?

HUGH: *(Reentering.)* Three brandies. Thomson.

HUGH hands brandies to WINNIE and THOMSON.

MARIE: Winnie thinks she's going to put the peas over there.

HUGH: Damn good place for them. Just don't plant squash. Disgusting vegetable.

WINNIE: What's your favourite vegetable, Mr. Thomson?

Thunder. THOMSON watches the sky.

WINNIE: Tom?

THOMSON: …Pardon?

The TRAINORS exchange looks.

MARIE: …Are you feeling quite well, Mr. Thomson?

THOMSON: …Uh, yes—fine.

MARTIN BLETCHER enters, tentatively.

BLETCHER: Mrs. Trainor. Mr. Trainor.

MARIE: Oh—hello, Martin.

HUGH: Bleacher.

BLETCHER: Bletcher. Evening, Winnie. Thomson. Planting your garden?

WINNIE: What do you think, Martin—peas over there, or over there?

BLETCHER looks around awkwardly, afraid it may be a trick question.

BLETCHER: Don't you always put the peas over there?

MARIE: Exactly! Thank you, Martin.

BLETCHER: Good drainage over there. Good drainage is always good for peas.

WINNIE: *(Indicating somewhere else.)* So, peas over there, I think.

HUGH: So, Tom, much money in painting?

MARIE: Hugh! What kind of question is that?!

HUGH: A damn straight forward one.

THOMSON: No. Not much.

HUGH: No. Wouldn't have thought so. I expect you have to be dead first.

MARIE: Hugh Trainor!

HUGH: Well, isn't that the way of the world?

WINNIE: I'm sure Mr. Thomson isn't concerned about the money, father. He's interested in the art.

THOMSON: I'd love to make money at it. Some people do.

HUGH: So, how do you make a living?

WINNIE: He draws pictures for the Eaton's Catalogue.

MARIE: The Eaton's Catalogue? No! The Eaton's Catalogue?

THOMSON: During the winter I work for a commercial art firm in Toronto.

MARIE: But we *love* the Eaton's Catalogue! You must be very talented!

BLETCHER: I use the Eaton's catalogue. …You know where.

BLETCHER snorts at his little joke. No one else seems all that amused.

HUGH: …So you make enough in the winter to support yourself in the park all summer?

MARIE: Oh, do stop badgering Mr. Thomson about money, Hugh. Surely there are more pleasant things we can talk about. Let's see: are you married, Mr. Thomson?

A crack of thunder disturbs THOMSON.

MARIE: …Are you sure you're feeling alright?

THOMSON continues to stare up at the sky, distracted.

THOMSON: No. I mean, no, I'm not married. Although…I proposed once. In Seattle. I was twenty-seven. She was fifteen, the daughter of a minister. And she laughed at me.

ALICE LAMBERT is heard more than seen, laughing a delightful young laugh.

She asked me—Alice was her name—she said, would I paint her in the nude, and I said, no, of course I won't, what would your father say? And she said…

ALICE: Why should you care what my father says?

THOMSON: But I did care. And besides, I was a letterman, not an artist. She wanted to write novels.

ALICE: Scandalous ones! With lots of plot!

THOMSON: I left Seattle the next day. Alice Lambert. And you know what she does now? She writes novels… Look at that grey!

MARIE: Pardon?

THOMSON: The sky.

MARIE: …Yes. The sky. Very nice.

THOMSON: It keeps…changing.

MARIE: Hugh, there is something very odd about that man.

HUGH: He's probably wondering what the hell we're doing out here when it's gonna piss down rain any second. I'm uncomfortable enough all week at the mill. I'm going inside. Marie?

MARIE: Yes, perhaps we should. And Martin. You will join us for dinner, won't you? Winnifred does so enjoy your company.

BLETCHER: Well, as a matter of fact... Yes. Thank you, Mrs. Trainor.

MARIE: Just give me a minute to set an extra place.

MARIE exits into the house.

WINNIE: ...I should have some seed markers.

BLETCHER: I've got some at the cabin. I could be back in...

WINNIE: Thank you, Martin.

BLETCHER starts to leave, then wonders if he's been conned somehow. He goes reluctantly.

I don't believe I've ever met someone like you.

THOMSON: I'm sorry. I shouldn't have talked about those things.

WINNIE: I found it very interesting.

THOMSON is staring at the sky again.

...It's so still. The calm before the storm.

Thunder.

ALICE: We'd make a terrible married couple.

WINNIE: ...Every year we set up the garden the same way. And it's always been just vegetables. Maybe this year some flowers.

Another crack of thunder; THOMSON again eyes the skies.

ALICE: Good-bye, Tom.

THOMSON: ...I should go.

WINNIE: But you haven't had dinner.

THOMSON: I have to try and get that grey.

WINNIE: Tonight's no night to be on the lake. You know enough to be careful, I hope.

THOMSON: Yes.

Another burst of thunder. BLETCHER re-enters.

BLETCHER: Got the seed markers.

THOMSON: ...Good night.

WINNIE: Good night, Mr. Thomson.

THOMSON exits. MARIE re-enters.

MARIE: Dinner's on. Martin?

BLETCHER: Thank you, Mrs. Trainor.

WINNIE: I'll be right there.

BLETCHER exits. MARIE looks around for THOMSON.

MARIE: Is that him in the canoe?

WINNIE: He has to try and get that grey.

MARIE: On a night like this? Are you certain about this man, Winnie? He seems so...passionate.

WINNIE: I would have thought passion was a good quality in a man.

MARIE: Only if it's directed at us, dear. ...Well, I can't say

I'm unhappy he's gone.

WINNIE: Yes, Mother. But he'll be back.

MARIE: Don't the dangerous ones always come back. Do come inside, Winnie. It's going to pour like judgment day.

MARIE exits. WINNIE watches THOMSON, then exits herself.

Scene 10—Thunderhead

Canoe Lake. Thunder. THOMSON, in a canoe, fights the elements.

"Thunderhead"

THOMSON: Lightning,
Rain.
Power.
Pain.
Cold front, increased wind
Clouds caught in the east wind
Thunderhead.

Captive.
Strange.
Colours
Change.
Gold cracks of lightning
Throat cold dry and tight'ning.
Thunderhead.

Hear the crack, then the shimmer then the buzz.
See the sky and the light that never was.
Everywhere, the air is trembling,
Shadows freeze,
Danger runs like whisper through the trees.

Glowing.

Clear.
Fury.
Fear.
Wind I can run with
Dark-souled sky I'm one with
Thunderhead.
Thunderhead…

Music continues. THOMSON has increasing trouble keeping afloat. Suddenly his canoe capsizes. He is in trouble in the water when DIXON appears out of nowhere, reaching for THOMSON from shore.

DIXON: Here, lad—reach!

DIXON grabs THOMSON's hand and brings him to safety.

Dammit, fella! You tryin' to kill yourself out there?!

THOMSON is exhausted and frightened, but he can't seem to keep his eyes off the storm.

We better get you somewhere outta the rain. My shack's not too far from here.

THOMSON: No. My pack.

DIXON: Forget that, what we need's kindling for a fire. Get you dried off.

THOMSON: No!

THOMSON sees his pack and scrambles to open it. He pulls out a "board" and paints. As the storm continues, He starts to sketch. His hands are obviously freezing, but he works on. DIXON can't believe what he's seeing.

VOICES: Hear the crack, then the shimmer then the buzz.
See the sky and the light that never was.
Everywhere, the air is trembling,

Shadows freeze…

THOMSON is unhappy with his attempt at capturing the storm.

THOMSON: You want kindling—here's kindling! A whole pack full of kindling!

THOMSON hands DIXON the board, and a number of boards from inside his pack. But then he starts painting again. DIXON admires the boards.

DIXON: Hey, these oughta burn real good!

THOMSON paints.

VOICES: Danger runs like whisper through the trees.

THOMSON & VOICES: Glowing.
Clear.
Fury.
Fear.
Wind I can run with
Dark-souled sky I'm one with
Thunderhead.
Thunderhead.
Thunderhead.

THOMSON finishes his painting in a wild fury.

Scene 11—Poachers I Didn't Already Know

In the bush. ROBINSON appears with his diary; DIXON sets up his trap.

ROBINSON: That first spring, 1912, I used to stumble across Tom in the bush the odd time—part of my job being to look for poachers. Poachers I didn't already know, that is. …Afternoon, Larry.

Caught by surprise, DIXON has his trap shut on his hand.

DIXON: Ah! …Oh. Robinson.

ROBINSON: Out for a stroll, are you?

DIXON: That's it. Out for a stroll. …Poaching's illegal.

ROBINSON: I know that.

DIXON: But if I see anyone—poaching—I'll sure tell one o' you rangers.

ROBINSON: Appreciate it, Larry.

DIXON: 'Though now come to think of it, there is that new fella I seen around. Tall. Suspicious lookin'.

ROBINSON: Suspicious?

DIXON: Shifty. Takes these bits of board, and dabs specks of paint on 'em. I don't know what he's doing but he's worth watching anyway.

ROBINSON: Well, is he an artist?

DIXON: A what?

ROBINSON: An artist.

DIXON: What the hell kind of a thing is that?

ROBINSON: *(To the audience.)* So I tried my best to explain to him what an artist is.

DIXON: Well, I don't know 'bout none of that, but I'd watch him anyways. It's no accounts like that don't leave no rabbits for the rest of us.

THOMSON enters, staring intently at something. DIXON and ROBINSON try to determine what it is that THOMSON is looking at.

…We call it—a pine tree. …Billions o' them jack

pines in this park. And they all look exactly like that one. *(Exits)*

ROBINSON: We'd had artists in the Park before—Tom never claimed to be the first—but there weren't many who as much as made the place home. Not that he was any expert that first year.

THOMSON: Look at that brown.

ROBINSON: I'd help him out when I could.

THOMSON: In that bush.

ROBINSON: *(Correcting him.)* "Fern". Osmunda fern. Turns that shade after the first frost. And in return, more often than not, he'd try to give me what he called his boards.

THOMSON hands ROBINSON a sketch. MARIE enters.

The longer he stayed, the less folks knew what to make of him. There was one day he near scared Winnie's mother half to death, came storming into her kitchen.

THOMSON and ROBINSON enter MARIE's kitchen.

THOMSON: I need a swamp! Dirty. Swampy. With those things that stick up. And greys! Everywhere different greys!

ROBINSON: She thought a minute, and suggested he try the little lake…

MARIE: …Marsh Hare, in behind the old timber camp.

ROBINSON: And without so much as a goodbye…

THOMSON storms off again, but not before perfunctorily handing ROBINSON another board.

MARIE: Without so much as a goodbye. You ask me, Mark Robinson, that man's demented.

DIXON re-enters.

ROBINSON: Popular opinion ran pretty much with Winnie's mother.

DIXON: Pixilated.

ROBINSON: Moonstruck, they said.

MARIE: Crazy as a North Bay coot.

DIXON: …Either that or a very smart poacher.

DIXON and MARIE exit.

ROBINSON: …I don't think folks 'round here ever really understood Tom. Always seemed to me there was only one place a person got to know the real Thomson. 'Cause if he was never very happy with his painting, he sure was proud of one thing.

ROBINSON joins THOMSON in a canoe.

Scene 12—The Baron

On Canoe Lake. Water, wind, birds. THOMSON and ROBINSON in a canoe, fishing.

THOMSON: *(Listening.)* Ruby-crowned Kinglet.

ROBINSON: *(Listens.)* Could be. Prefer the Grosbeak myself.

THOMSON: Cretin. *(Listens again.)* White-throated Sparrow.

ROBINSON listens again and there is the faint far-off sound of rustling in the trees, a snap, then a scream.

ROBINSON: Larry Dixon settin' illegal trap-lines. Good thing for him it's my day off.

Another silence.

THOMSON: Catbird… Warbler… Veery.

ROBINSON: Plenty of birds. Just no fish.

THOMSON looks uncomfortable.

THOMSON: Sure is a lotta water out here… Shouldn't've had that second cup of coffee.

THOMSON starts to stand up.

ROBINSON: Christmas, Tom—you're not gonna do that here? Nobody ever tell you standin' up in a canoe is about the stupidest thing you can do?

THOMSON stands, and the canoe rolls a bit. He turns and pees into the water.

…It's a verifiable fact that the majority of drowned canoe fishermen are found with their flies open.

THOMSON: *(Finished.)* But at least they died comfortable. *(Listens.)* Peeper frog.

THOMSON re-settles himself and starts to put the new lure on his line.

ROBINSON: Gonna paint today?

THOMSON: Too green. Green is boring as hell. Early Spring and Fall's the time to paint.

ROBINSON: Meanin' you're too lazy… Where'd you get the lures?

THOMSON: My bugs? Painted 'em myself. You like 'em?

ROBINSON: Never was much for the "Hot Mush" school of fish lures. *(Pauses, thinks, then laughs.)* Hey, I think I made a joke.

THOMSON: Your fishing's the joke, Robinson.

ROBINSON: No, I did! Hot Mush *school of lures*?

THOMSON: You've been out in the sun too long.

ROBINSON: No sense of humour.

Having finished putting the new lure on his line, THOMSON casts off again.

THOMSON: Now we'll catch some fish.

ROBINSON: Soon as I get my line in.

ROBINSON casts, and again there is a silence.

THOMSON: These fish are the real critics. They take one look at my lure, see all there is to see, then calmly swim away.

ROBINSON: Seen the Baron lately?

THOMSON: Had 'im over for dinner last week.

ROBINSON: No! The Baron?

THOMSON: Said to say hello.

ROBINSON: Anybody ever does catch the Baron it sure won't be some city-boy.

THOMSON: Had 'im on the line, had 'im a yard from the net!

ROBINSON: No kidding!

THOMSON: Coulda counted his fin stripes!

ROBINSON: So?

THOMSON: Damn thing winked at me, tossed his head and disappeared.

ROBINSON: Fish don't wink. They got no eyelids! You'd know that if you ever caught one.

THOMSON: He winked in recognition of me as a fellow artist.

ROBINSON: Artist, my aspidistra! The Baron is a Ranger! Superior survival skills!

THOMSON: Somewhere in the murkiness of this water lurks the Baron. And I want the Baron!

A tug on THOMSON's line. Both men are suddenly alert.

Shit!

ROBINSON: Tom, you got somethin'!

The "fish" pulls mightily on the line.

Christmas, it's a big one!

THOMSON: *(Battles the fish.)* It is the Baron!

ROBINSON: I can't see. Bring it closer.

The battle continues. THOMSON reels it closer still.

Well, I'll be jiggered! Could be!

THOMSON: I got 'im! I got 'im!!

ROBINSON: A little more!

The Baron escapes.

THOMSON: No!

ROBINSON: He's gone?

THOMSON: Damn!

ROBINSON: You had 'im!

THOMSON: I had 'im!

ROBINSON: I couldn't tell if it was the Baron or not.

THOMSON: Damn!

ROBINSON: No sense getting mad—there's no way of knowing if it was even him.

THOMSON: I know. Why do you think I'm mad?

"The One That Got Away"

Sure I can paint
But to tell the truth
That ain't saying much.
'Cause there is an art form
With a far tougher touch.
Rembrandt was an genius,
But let there be no doubt,
The real art in nature
Is reelin' in a trout.

Yes, I'm endowed
With a talent
But I'm prouder by far
Of all of my masterpieces
Landing Arctic char.

ROBINSON: I've caught perch and goldeye
From the Soo to Hudson's Bay,
But oh Irene
You should've seen
The one that got away!

BOTH: You should've seen the one that got away!
Second to none,
It must've weighed a ton.
And if it takes till my dying day
I'm gonna get the one that got away!

ROBINSON: Now when a thing
Comes too easily
It brings on the thought,
That clever it may be,
But important it's not.
And if poor Michelangelo
Had one unanswered wish,

He'd say, "Why hast thou forsaken me,
Dear God, why can't I fish?!"

Of course, he'd say it in Italian.

BOTH: You should've seen the one that got away!
I'd give up Rome
To bring that sucker home.
And if it takes till my dying day
I'm gonna get the one that got away!

There is a tug on ROBINSON's line.

ROBINSON: Hey, now I got one!

In no time at all, ROBINSON reels in a trout.

ROBINSON: Now that's fishing!

THOMSON: It's not the Baron.

ROBINSON: No, it's better. It's dinner.

BOTH: The fish we catch are tasty
But the aftertaste is always rather thin
'Cause the one we'll hunger for all our lives
Is the one we couldn't reel in.

Yes, you should've seen the one that got away!
Oh, what a loss—
At least this big across!
And if it takes till my dying day
I'm gonna brook no more delay—
I'm gonna get the one that got away!

They laugh and celebrate their catch.

Scene 13—Larry Dixon Splitting Wood

DIXON outside his shack, with hat and axe.

DIXON: This here behind me's my shack. You probably recognize it... 'Course, you prob'ly recognize me for that matter... The hat—the axe?

He bends over in the pose of "Larry Dixon Splitting Wood".

"Larry Dixon Splitting Wood", right? I knew you'd recognize me eventually. Hell, if I hadn't been in a private collection all them years I guess I'd be as famous as them jack pines he kept doin'.

Folks say—artsy folks, anyway—that Tom wasn't all that good at paintin' people. That could be — don't really have an opinion on that. Don't know much about art, just know I like to be painted. Built this shack myself. Wasn't much. Wasn't ever meant to be. Annie Fraser come by one night —not for what you think, though some did—told me it had—what did she say?—"potential". Hell. What it had was more drafts than conscription and the plumbing quarter mile up the path. But this one Spring, Tom brought this fella Lismer. And one day, when I guess this Lismer was tired o' trampin' through the woods fightin' 'squiters, he sat down and done this picture o' my shack. He actually took the time and painted a picture o' my shack. Hell, I laughed for a week. Couldn't poach for laughin' gave me away! Some joke!

Then a couple o' months later I heard he'd sold the damn thing for four hundred dollars. Four hundred dollars for a picture o' my shack. Well, I didn't know whether to laugh or cry. Some jack-ass city-slicker pays four hundred dollars to put a paintin' o' Larry Dixon's shack—oh, sorry, "The Guide's Home"—on their wall. Hell, I woulda sold 'em the whole damn shack for less than that.

Never did make much sense to me. Just goes to show ya, I guess, ya never know what's got "potential."

He leans over again as in "Larry Dixon Splitting Wood", holds the pose a moment then holds his hand out, grinning.

DIXON: "Larry Dixon Splitting Wood". Four hundred dollars, please.

Laughing at his terrific joke, hje begins to exit. THOMSON hands him a copy of "Larry Dixon Splitting Wood" before he goes.

Scene 14—The Undisputed Champeen of Algonquin Park

Mowat Lodge. A waltz is playing. ANNIE is setting up for a party. SHANNON enters behind her and sweeps her into a waltz.

ANNIE: You waltz divinely, Mr. Fraser.

SHANNON: And you, Mrs. Fraser, are as comely a colleen as ever a moon painted gold.

ANNIE: You used to say those things and mean them.

SHANNON: I was an idiot boy once to be sure.

ANNIE: I liked that idiot boy.

She stops dancing and gives him a small wrapped parcel.

Happy Birthday, Shannon.

SHANNON: *(Genuinely touched.)* Annie. Thank you.

He opens the package and takes out a small set of hand-painted wind chimes.

ANNIE: They're wind chimes. Every time you hear them you can think of me.

SHANNON: Hand-painted.

ANNIE: …Yes.

SHANNON: Thomson's a good teacher.

ANNIE: *(Kisses him.)* Happy Birthday.

WINNIE and MARIE enter.

WINNIE: Here they are.

MARIE: The returns of the day, Shannon. These must be the famous wind-chimes.

SHANNON: You heard then, Mrs. T., that my Annie's taking art lessons?

MARIE: I did, yes.

SHANNON: Where is Tom, so I can thank him, too?

SHANNON moves to hang up the wind-chimes. BLETCHER enters with a cup of punch in each hand and hurries to WINNIE.

BLETCHER: I brought you some punch, Winnie.

WINNIE: ...Thank you, Martin.

MacCALLUM and THOMSON enter with punch; THOMSON has two glasses. An awkward moment as THOMSON sees that WINNIE has been given a glass by BLETCHER. He turns to ANNIE.

THOMSON: ...Annie Fraser—fresh punch.

MacCALLUM offers his punch to MARIE.

MacCALLUM: ...Mrs. Trainor.

MARIE: How gallant, good sir. ...I understand you're feeling better, Doctor.

MacCALLUM: Please—it's Jim. And yes, there may be some rough magic in this Park air after all. The curse of good health may force me to leave you all sooner than I had begun to hope.

MARIE: So you and Tom will *both* be returning to Toronto.

This appears to be news to everyone but WINNIE.

MacCALLUM: …I didn't know about Tom.

THOMSON: Yes. Enough time wasted here.

MacCALLUM: On your painting.

THOMSON: …I'm a commercial artist, not a painter. Time to get back to that.

BLETCHER: They need you to do those Eaton's catalogues, do they?

THOMSON: I need the job.

SHANNON: Well, this is a surprise. But then what's a birthday for if not for pleasant surprises.

ANNIE: Shannon…

SHANNON: Still, no doubt he's lookin' forward to goin' back down the city, bein' with his high-class friends again. I expect Martin's lookin' forward to it at any rate.

ANNIE: Please, Shannon…

SHANNON: Am I not only sayin' what's true? Not that we won't miss you, o' course, Tom. The rent on the room, anyway. *(Laughs.)*

MacCALLUM: Mrs Trainor, have you seen the painting Tom did of the Mowat?

MARIE: I don't believe I have.

MacCALLUM: I convinced Mrs. Fraser to hang it in the parlor. Perhaps you'd let me show you.

MARIE: Yes.

MacCALLUM: If you'd care to join us, Tom, there's something we might discuss.

THOMSON: Of course.

SHANNON: That's right, Tommy. Off you go. Out of harm's

way. Leave Martin and I to have some real fun on our own. What do you say, Martin—how about you and me have a little arm wrestle? See if you've improved any.

BLETCHER: No.

SHANNON: I'll represent our Canadian boys in France and you can fight for your beloved Germans.

BLETCHER: I'm an American.

SHANNON: Martin and his German ancestry don't believe the Allies have a chance.

BLETCHER: Thousands of Canadians killed already. A waste of good men.

THOMSON: Brave men dying for a just cause.

BLETCHER: Though I note, Thomson, that you're here.

SHANNON: Tom tried to enlist, didn't you, Tom. What was it—flat feet?

THOMSON: What about you, Bletcher? You brave enough to fight?

BLETCHER: As an American, I have no need. It isn't our conflict.

THOMSON: Not yet.

BLETCHER: Not ever. Americans are smart enough to stay out of something that isn't our business.

THOMSON: But are they smart enough to fly a flag properly? You raise that Stars and Stripes outside your cabin again, you remember to fly the Union Jack over top!

BLETCHER: Or what? Some coward comes in the middle of the night again and cuts it down?

THOMSON: Wouldn't be surprised.

SHANNON: Now, boys. It's not that I wouldn't relish a good fisticuffs, but if anyone is going to enjoy a good knock-down on my birthday it's me. Now as undisputed champeen of Algonquin Park, I am duty bound to put my title on the line as often as possible. C'mon, Martin, roll up your sleeves.

BLETCHER: I said, no.

THOMSON: Besides, Shannon, Martin being a policeman, he could probably break your arm if he wanted to.

BLETCHER: I'm not a policeman. I'm an investigator.

SHANNON: Sure, sure, Martin, we know that. Private investigator. Like Sherlock Holmes.

BLETCHER: No.

SHANNON: Peeping through transoms at husbands sneaking a little on the side.

BLETCHER: What I do is good, honest work. Though I see enough men who don't.

THOMSON: Meaning who?

BLETCHER: Meaning men who'd rather find a woman to live off than do any real work of their own. Gigolos, they're called. And worse. Itinerant actors. Misunderstood artists.

SHANNON: Go get him, Martin.

MARIE, ANNIE, WINNIE and MacCALLUM have by now reentered.

MARIE: I'm sure Martin didn't mean that the way it sounded.

SHANNON: You don't think so, Mrs T.?

ANNIE: Besides, this isn't the time for this.

SHANNON: Annie's right. This is a party. Let's arm wrestle! How 'bout you, Thomson? You've never challenged the champ.

THOMSON: I wouldn't presume.

ANNIE: Did you bring your mandolin, Tom?

THOMSON: I did.

ANNIE: Play something we can dance to.

SHANNON: Sure, that's better. No arm-wrestling for Thomson. He might sprain a wrist, and poor Tommy if he couldn't lift that great big heavy paint brush and dab those little bitty specks of paint all day.

ANNIE: Shannon!

SHANNON and THOMSON stare at one another as WINNIE brings THOMSON his mandolin.

WINNIE: *(Privately.)* Here, Tom.

THOMSON: I'll wrestle you.

SHANNON: Alright! Set it up, Annie! Now we'll see something, eh, Martin? Good to know there's at least some of us here don't back down from a fight!

ANNIE is reluctant to set up for the arm-wrestle. BLETCHER and THOMSON carry on despite her. A table is secured, or a stool on a bench. THOMSON and SHANNON prepare.

ANNIE: You don't have to do this, Tom.

SHANNON: Ah, now, Annie—give the city boy a chance to prove his mettle before we send him home to momma! Let's go—I'll be the north bush and you be the greenhorn.

SHANNON offers his arm, then is surprised when THOMSON offers his left hand. But SHANNON gamely matches THOMSON's choice.

SHANNON: Martin?

BLETCHER: Ready? And… Go.

The arm-wrestling begins. It starts by appearing friendly, as SHANNON expects an easy victory. But as it becomes clearer that SHANNON is in for a fight, he starts to sweat. The others watch with interest, kibitzing.

WINNIE: …C'mon, Tom!

ANNIE: …That's it! That's it, yes!

WINNIE: …Get him, Tom!

Eventually, SHANNON wins—immediately in his glory.

SHANNON: Ahah! Winner and still undisputed champeen! Nice try, Tom.

THOMSON: Next time I'll use my good hand.

SHANNON: What?

THOMSON: Now I'll take my mandolin.

WINNIE gives THOMSON the mandolin.

SHANNON: What do you mean, your good hand?

THOMSON: I mean next time I'll wrestle you using my strong hand.

SHANNON: Use any hand you like! C'mon, again!

THOMSON turns to the MUSICIANS.

THOMSON: What'll it be, my friends? Something in a jig, maybe.

ANNIE: "Wildflowers".

THOMSON and the band start into a jig. WINNIE goes to BLETCHER to get him to dance. He resists.

"Wildflowers"

WINNIE: Well, there's them that likes a garden
With the flowers in a row,
And them that likes a river slow.
But then there's them the devil kissed
When they were but a child
Who like their water white
And their flowers wild.

Wildflowers
Growing where they will
Reveling in the meadows,
Trumpeting up the hill.
Lay down the rake,
And lay down the hoe
Let the wildflowers grow!

WINNIE coaxes ANNIE into the song. SHANNON becomes increasingly annoyed.

ANNIE: Well, now
You can plant your flower seed
And weed it while it grows
And you may get the perfect rose.
But me, I hate
To cultivate
What's best left unbeguiled;
So give me something rampant, loud,
Tempestuous and wild.

ANNIE & WINNIE: Wildflowers
Rioting down the trail.
Fireweed and viper,
Thundering through the vale.
Show me the seed
The sou'wester will sow;
Yes, take me where the wildflowers grow!

WINNIE and ANNIE begin to dance as the music picks up in tempo. WINNIE dances with BLETCHER. ANNIE tries to get SHANNON to dance, but when he refuses to join her, she gets THOMSON to lay down his mandolin and dance. Eventually, ANNIE leaves THOMSON for SHANNON, and THOMSON ends up with WINNIE. BLETCHER isn't happy about that. The dance becomes increasingly uninhibited as THOMSON becomes the exuberant focal point with both ANNIE and WINNIE whirling around him. Both BLETCHER and SHANNON watch the joyful and sensuous dance with growing anxiety and impatience. Finally SHANNON goes and pulls ANNIE away from TOM.

SHANNON: What the hell are you doing, Annie?!

The music stops.

ANNIE: What did it look like I was doing?! I was having fun for a change!

SHANNON: You're acting a damn fool! And as for you, Thomson, I'll thank you in future to keep your hands off my wife!

WINNIE: I think we should go, Tom.

SHANNON: No, not before he fights me with his "good hand". He's not going to make an ass outta me that easy.

THOMSON: C'mon, Winnie.

THOMSON turns his back to leave, not seeing SHANNON about to attack him.

SHANNON: Thomson!

WINNIE: Tom, look out!

THOMSON turns just in time to avoid the SHANNON's blow and manages quickly to turn the attack against SHANNON. SHANNON is at THOMSON's mercy. But despite his extraordinary anger THOMSON gets his temper under control.

THOMSON: This is my good hand, Fraser.

HE pushes SHANNON the floor and exits. WINNIE tries to follow THOMSON but is prevented by MARIE.

MARIE: Winnie...

MARIE leads WINNIE off. ANNIE exits after them , upset. MacCALLUM follows THOMSON. BLETCHER goes to the defeated SHANNON.

BLETCHER: ...Happy Birthday, Shannon.

BLETCHER exits, striking the wind-chimes on his way out. SHANNON stops the wind-chimes angrily, looks off after THOMSON, then exits.

Scene 15—Even More Out Of Control

In the trees. THOMSON appears, still angry. MacCALLUM follows him on.

MacCALLUM: Tom...! Tom! Slow down, for god's sake. I've barely survived one illness, now you're going to give me a heart attack.

THOMSON: Go back to the Mowat, Doctor.

MacCALLUM: And let you go back to being a fool.

THOMSON: How am I a fool?

MacCALLUM: I could recite the list but I'm afraid I don't have that long to live. Let me waste what little breath I have left and tell you why I risked my life to follow you here. You've heard of the Ontario Society of Artists Annual Exhibit of new work? ...Most of the boys exhibit a piece or two every year. Harris, Lismer, Jackson.

THOMSON: I'll buy a ticket one year.

MacCALLUM: I've written to Harris about you. Sent him a couple of your pieces.

THOMSON: To Lawren Harris?!

MacCALLUM: He had one hung at the OSA.

THOMSON: No.

MacCALLUM: Yes.

THOMSON: Which one?

MacCALLUM: "Northern Lake".

THOMSON: Doctor, you had no right to send…! And…?

MacCALLUM: …There were a few comments, of course.

THOMSON: Like what? What comments?

MacCALLUM: Well—that—perhaps—it wasn't completely under control…

THOMSON: What does that mean!? Not "completely under control"?! Damn critics wouldn't know a real goddam painting if it came up and kicked them in the goddam ass!

MacCALLUM: It sold.

THOMSON: …What?!

MacCALLUM: To Her Majesty's Loyal Government of Ontario.

THOMSON: …For how much?

MacCALLUM: Two hundred and fifty dollars. I took the liberty of bringing you the cheque.

THOMSON takes the cheque from MacCALLUM and starts to leave.

...One last thing. I made a proposal to Alex Jackson last year. He accepted and I hope you'll do the same. I'd like to guarantee your expenses for the period of one year, if you'll devote that year to painting.

THOMSON: ...You want to pay me to paint?

MacCALLUM: You won't get rich from it. Enough to cover supplies, basic living expenses.

THOMSON: No. I won't waste your money.

MacCALLUM: This isn't charity. I consider it an investment. Frankly, if it had been me rather than the OSA selling that painting, we'd have made far more than two hundred and fifty. ...Besides, I rather like the idea of letting you get things even more "out of control". *(Holds out his hand.)* A year. Starting today.

THOMSON shakes his hand.

...Tom Thomson—painter!

MacCALLUM smiles and exits. THOMSON turns and takes in his surroundings, as exhilarated as he is apprehensive. The colours change.

"Northern River"

THOMSON: Standing in the shadows,
Looking towards the light
Wondering where the river goes.
Hovering on the water
Trees and sky unite
Flowing where the river flows.

Northern River
Can we ever know

Where these Northern Rivers
Colours in the Storm
Go?

Pine wood arms to hold me
Dark and cool and still
I'm frightened how the river burns.
Wind sweeps up behind me
Rustling down the hill
Drawn to where the river turns.

Northern River
Can we learn to read
Where these Northern Rivers
Lead?

Were I to step out of the trees
And dare the river
My face would ripple in the water
Open to the skies
And I would float
Like a seed in the wind
The colours on the river
The colours in my eyes.

Northern River
Dare we ever know
Where these Northern Rivers
Go?

Northern River
Changing greys and blue
Northern River
Take me with you.

THOMSON sees the park with new eyes.

Part Three—Daring The River

Scene 16—I Feel Like A Ghost To You?

THOMSON's campsite. WILD MARY enters, kerosene lamp in hand, and looks around. She spots some of his boards and starts rummaging through them. THOMSON is alarmed by her sudden appearance.

THOMSON: Who's there?

WILD MARY pays him little mind and continues going through the boards, quickly dismissing each one in turn. THOMSON approaches her.

What are you doing?! Be careful with those!

As he approaches, however, she suddenly hisses at him. He backs off and she resumes looking at the boards.

...Who are you?

Finally she finds one that catches her interest. She holds her lamp closer, allowing her a better look.

...Finally find one you like?

WILD MARY: Osmunda fern.

THOMSON: ...That's right.

WILD MARY: After the first frost.

THOMSON: How did you know that?

WILD MARY: 'Cause that's what the hell it looks like. I'll take this one.

She starts to leave.

THOMSON: Wait a minute—you can't just take it.

WILD MARY: You let Dixon take one. You give 'em to that Ranger!

THOMSON: Sure, but…

She tosses the board back.

WILD MARY: Then keep it. …Grey in the sky's all wrong anyway.

She starts to leave again.

THOMSON: Who are you?

WILD MARY: …That your canvas?

THOMSON: *(Puzzled.)* Canvas? No. *(Referring to his boards.)* I mean, one of them might make a canvas. If I decide to do it up later. But it's these first. Boards.

She points at THOMSON's tent.

WILD MARY: I said, is that your canvas? Pretending to be a tent?

THOMSON: *(Looking off, understanding.)* Oh. My tent. Yes.

WILD MARY: Better hope we don't get a wind. And I suppose ya call that a camp-fire.

THOMSON isn't sure what to say.

…Them your boots?

THOMSON: *(Looks at his boots, then at WILD MARY.)* Not the right boots?

She comes to THOMSON, examining him uncomfortably closely. She touches his face, and He flinches away from her hand.

WILD MARY: Some people think I'm a ghost. I feel like a ghost to you?

She grabs one of his hands and examines it, then the other, turning them over and holding them to the light. She touches his hand to her face, smiles oddly, then hisses at him again. Startled, he recoils from her. She laughs again softly and turns to leave. Just before she disappears entirely, she turns back to him.

Grey's all wrong, ain't it.

THOMSON looks at his board. Then when he looks back again for her, she's gone. He listens, unnerved, and settles in to guard himself against the night.

Scene 17—Doesn't Look Too Dangerous

ROBINSON consults his diary.

ROBINSON: 1915. I came across Thomson today at the edge of a river. "Where's this river run?" he said. I said, "Downstream." ...He didn't get it. "It's a joke," I said, "Bush humour." He just kept inching closer to the bank and I told him be careful, rivers run quick this time of year. "Doesn't look too dangerous," he said. I said, "Nothin' to do with how things look. There's guides lived here all their lives took one too many drinks, ended up drowning in six inches of warm water." Didn't know it then, but that's exactly what took Larry Dixon. I made a note, underlined it, to keep an eye on this Thomson; that if he wasn't careful...1915: "Doesn't look too dangerous," he said.

ROBINSON exits.

Scene 18 —That's What Makes It An Adventure

WINNIE joins THOMSON by a campfire. She wears a shawl against the coming night.

WINNIE: You fry a good trout, Mr. Thomson.

THOMSON: You *catch* a good trout, Miss Trainor.

WINNIE: Someday you'll catch one big enough to eat, too.

THOMSON smiles. A comfortable pause.

...Wild Mary.

THOMSON: What?

WINNIE: Your visitor the other night. Bit of a local legend. Lives in the bush, exactly where nobody seems to know for sure. Most people seem to think she died years ago. Do you believe in ghosts?

THOMSON: Not that carry kerosene lamps.

WINNIE: I don't believe in ghosts. If you meet her again be careful. She's been said to have done a lot wilder things than stealing paintings.

THOMSON: Like what?

WINNIE: I'm too much of a lady to say.

Another comfortable silence.

WINNIE: ...Tom—you started painting when?

THOMSON: Seriously? After I came to the park for the first time.

WINNIE: Three years ago. You were how old?

THOMSON: Thirty-five.

WINNIE: I'm thirty-five this year. ...It's been so warm it's nice to feel the wind. ...Tom—what's it feel like? When you paint.

THOMSON: ...Good. I dunno. Scary sometimes. ...I dunno.

WINNIE: Good but scary. ...When I was a kid, I used to explore the park by myself. Try to go into the trees as far from our cabin as I could. Each day a little farther. But when it felt scarier than good, I'd go home. Now I think about seeing the world. Africa. France.

THOMSON: Then you should go.

WINNIE drops the shawl from her shoulders.

You'll catch a chill.

He comes to her and touches her lightly. Nothing is said for a few moments.

WINNIE: ...I invited you for dinner last Saturday.

THOMSON: I went north. I thought I was only going for a couple of days. I'm sorry.

WINNIE: It's alright.

THOMSON: The colours...

WINNIE: You don't have to explain.

THOMSON: I'm glad I didn't forget today.

He moves closer to her.

WINNIE: Every year I'm more and more on time for everything. I hate that. ...You, on the other hand, are never on time for anything. You don't arrive at all if something better comes up.

THOMSON: Winnie, I'm sorry.

WINNIE: I like it that—that you're not run by what other people expect. That my mother thinks you're deranged. Sometimes I act a bit deranged myself just to drive her crazy. Maybe someday they'll be calling me Wild Winnie. ...Have I ever told you about Angus MacKensie? First man ever asked me to marry him. Said he'd take me anywhere in the world I wanted to go. He has five kids now... Did I ever mention Howard Schnieder?

THOMSON: No.

WINNIE: Best damn hockey player Huntsville ever produced. If I'd said yes to him I'd be living in Montreal now, in the biggest house you ever saw. But there was something else I thought I wanted.

THOMSON moves towards WINNIE, but she stops him.

Not some*one* A place. A feeling. It's like what always happens to me: I'll be doing something—something I do every day—when all of a sudden, like a tree when the wind changes, everything turns right around. And somehow out of nowhere I see things, things I know aren't really there.

THOMSON: They are there.

WINNIE: No. But I feel like the wind's gotten inside me somehow, and is churning around in there like in a pile of fallen leaves. And I feel—what? —exhilarated. For just a second. And then scared. And then it goes away. It always goes away.

THOMSON: ...It'll be dark soon. We should probably go.

WINNIE: Not yet.

THOMSON: Your parents won't be expecting you?

WINNIE: I came up by myself this weekend. ...There's a river runs off the lake not too far from here. Feel adventuresome?

THOMSON: What's down the river?

WINNIE: That's what makes it an adventure.

THOMSON: The water's not too fast?

WINNIE: For city folk, maybe.

THOMSON: ...Climb aboard.

WINNIE: After you.

They both stand near the stern of the canoe. THOMSON is perplexed that WINNIE is not climbing into the bow. She stands her ground, smiling at him.

THOMSON: I usually take the stern.

WINNIE: I know.

THOMSON: *(Points at the bow.)* But don't you think it would be better if you…?

WINNIE: No.

Again a stand-off at the stern. She continues to smile at him. At a loss, THOMSON gives in and moves to the bow. WINNIE pushes off and gets in herself. THOMSON is confused about his role; he doesn't know which side to paddle on. WINNIE enjoys his discomfort. WILD MARY and other SHADES have appeared behind them, watching.

"Still Waters/White Water"

WILD MARY /SHADES:
Still waters
Run deep, run deep.
Dark and silent,
With secrets to keep.
Motionless.
Fathomless.
Stirring from sleep In the deep of the still,
Still waters.

THOMSON: You're sure you feel comfortable back there?

They paddle on awhile.

WINNIE: The bow paddler doesn't try to steer.

THOMSON: Sorry.

WINNIE: Here's the river.

They negotiate the canoe into the river.

VOICES: Still waters
Run cold, run cold.
Blue to deep-green
To charcoal to gold.
Down like the well
Of the strongest will
Run the still,
Run the still, still waters.

THOMSON: You're a remarkable woman. You're wasted as a bookkeeper. You should be—what? what do remarkable women become?—a novelist, a suffragette. A world traveler charting unexplored wilderness.

THOMSON is enjoying himself. With his back to WINNIE, however, he doesn't realize how it's affecting her.

What do you want to be, Winnie? What do you wish for on falling stars?

Her silence causes THOMSON to turn to look at her.

You ignoring me?

WINNIE: Watch the water.

THOMSON: The current's getting stronger. You do know this river, don't you?

WINNIE: The trick is not to be pulled along. The trick is to be in control.

THOMSON: And you're in control?

WINNIE: There's no fun in being too much in control.

VOICES: Deep into the canyon
Where it never sees the sun
Silent runs the bright
White water!

Never far from danger,
And yet never far from shore,
Hungry roars the bite
Of white water!

THOMSON: Maybe we shouldn't do this.

WINNIE: Keep the bow away from the pull.

THOMSON: Winnie…

WINNIE: Don't be such a bookkeeper, Mr Thomson.

THOMSON's eyes widen at the coming water. WINNIE is determined.

THOMSON: Oh shit.

The ride gets rougher. They concentrate on keeping the canoe under control.

You have shot rapids before? There's an eddy—we could make for that.

WINNIE: No.

THOMSON: Oh shit!

The ride gets rougher yet.

VOICES: Scampering,
Thundering,
Bursting like a cloud-burst,
Coursing like the damned and cursed.
Willowing,
Plummeting,
The palette and the palette knife run spinning into
White.
White
Water!

THOMSON: There's a tree…!

WINNIE: Back ferry! Draw left!

THOMSON tries to follow instructions. He also starts to enjoy himself.

THOMSON: Whoa! Missed it! Hold on! Rocks either side!

They are swept between rocks, pulled forward.

Yes!

WINNIE: Deeper water right!

THOMSON: I'm with you.

WINNIE: Let it drift!

THOMSON: This is *not* drifting! Hold on!

VOICES: Churning like a timber-run,
The crush of rock and bark,
Liquid sparks ignite
White water.
Pounding like the mill-stone,
Seething like the wheel
Haunted squeals incite
The white water!

They shoot the worst of it, rocking and rolling madly. But they come out the other end, none the worse—at least physically—for wear.

THOMSON: I can't believe we made it!

WINNIE: Pull us over.

THOMSON: Not yet.

WINNIE: I have to check my paddle. Pull us into shore.

THOMSON: Aye, aye, Captain.

THOMSON pulls them to shore. He gets out and helps WINNIE out.

You're some pilot! Let's go have a look. At what we just ran. I want to see it from shore.

WINNIE: You go ahead.

THOMSON: You alright?

WINNIE: I'm fine. Go have your look. Paint me a picture.

THOMSON: ...That's exactly what it feels like, Winnie. That's exactly what it feels like to paint!

THOMSON exits. WINNIE's composure begins to crack. She looks back up the river.

VOICES: Still waters
Run deep, run deep.
Dark and silent,
With secrets to keep.
No colour.
All colours.
Stirring.
Asleep.
Deep run the still, still waters.

WINNIE shivers involuntarily, a look of abject terror mixed suddenly with relief and elation. She freezes when THOMSON speaks; he has obviously been watching her.

THOMSON: The moon's bright tonight. Look at the light on the water. ...It looks like one colour—but it's dozens of colours. Can you see them?

WINNIE: And what do you see when you look at me? How many colours?

THOMSON: We shouldn't canoe home in the dark.

WINNIE: ...No.

THOMSON: We'll watch the colours change on the water. The colour of everything changes all the time, you know.

WINNIE laughs.

...What?

WINNIE: Everyone thinks you're crazy.

THOMSON: What about you?

WINNIE: I'm not crazy.

THOMSON pushes WINNIE "to the precipice".

THOMSON: Winnie Trainor—you could be crazier than you think.

"Comes The Time"

WINNIE: Comes the time
When the maple bleeds the red into green.
Comes the time
When the autumn colours roar.
Comes the day
When the timber dam breaks way
And the freed water
Overflows the shoreline.

COMPANY: Comes the night
When the autumn moon lies nested in stars
Full of gold, full of longing,
Full of pain.
Comes the blue
As the morning rivers through
And the new blossoms open to the rain.

To everything there is a season,
To some it's Spring, to some it's fall.
And like every tree
Has roots we cannot see
So may we have strengths we've never seen at all.

Then comes the leap
As the salmon fights the current for home.
Comes the sweep as the young hawk starts to climb.
Comes the moment when suddenly we'll know
To be ready when it comes, comes the time.

To be ready when it comes, comes the time.

The colours change. THOMSON and WINNIE are full of all the possibilities of the future.

End of Act I.

Act II

Scene 19—I'm The Guide, Ain't I?

ROBINSON consults his diary.

ROBINSON: 1917. Tom's last year in the park. "The flies have been as bad this Spring as most of us can ever remember." …There have been a lot of theories about what happened to Tom that year. Suicide. Murder. Run off to "parts unknown." But I suppose "being drove crazy by flies" is as good as any of them.

ROBINSON watches as FRANCES McGILLVRAY appears, a "city-woman" in her fifties. She doesn't look properly dressed for a trek through the bush, but She is obviously determined. She looks around at everything with great interest and intensity. DIXON then appears, waving to FRANCES to follow him. They circle closer to THOMSON's campsite, although DIXON seems not exactly sure where he is. FRANCES watches him dubiously. They slap the odd black fly during their conversation.

FRANCES: You're certain you know how to find him?

DIXON: I'm the guide, ain't I?

FRANCES: ...Have you known Tom long?

DIXON: Ever since he started comin' up here. *(Calculating.)* Five years now. Taught him everything he knows about the bush. Never seen you here before though.

FRANCES: No. This is my first trip. It's beautiful.

DIXON: Looks that way in pictures, I guess. ...Expectin' ya, is he? You his mother?

FRANCES: ...I'm a colleague. From Toronto. Are we almost there?

DIXON: This is it.

She looks around uncertainly.

FRANCES: This is where he lives?

DIXON: Has been. Got a few favourite spots. But this year's been here mostly.

FRANCES: Will he be back soon, do you think?

DIXON: A few minutes, maybe. Or a few weeks.

FRANCES: A few weeks?

DIXON: Never know with Thomson. A few needles short of a pine some days—if you know what I mean.

DIXON imitates THOMSON checking his boards against "Nature".

(As THOMSON.) "Damn! That's not…! God-damn! Why can't I get that mother-lovin' bejesus grey?!" *(To FRANCES.)* Thomson. "Artistic distemper'ment", they call it. Been gettin' that way a lot this Spring. But, hell, it ain't what most folks think. Bit off more than he can spit, has Tom. You probably ain't noticed, seein' you just met me—but, fact is, Tom kinda tries to be a lot like me. And—well—gives him a lot to live up to. Weren't long after he first came up here, he took out a guide's licence—like I had. A dollar a year. Even did some fire-rangering one summer. And over the years, well, Tom's sorta begun to fit in. And this damn place has started to drive him just as loco as it's drove the rest of us.

"The Algonquin Breakdown"

DIXON: Algonquin is a paradise,
You city folk all know:
A place you see in paintin's,
But never dare to go.
The winter snow,
The leaves of fall,
Them summer birds that sing;
But most of all Algonquin is:
The black flies in the Spring.

He starts to slap at some black flies, getting more and more animated. The number develops into a step dance as a result of DIXON's slapping of the black flies.

Well, Greece has got them statues,
And London got Big Ben,
And Paris got them night clubs
If a fella gets the yen.

And somewhere called Arabia
Has magic flyin' rugs,
But here we got billions
Of blood-suckin' bugs!

It's the Algonquin Breakdown!
When something I can't hardly see
Drives me near out of my tree.
The Algonquin Breakdown!
Damned if a bug ain't made a monkey outta me!

Well, you can bring mosquito nets
And bug dope by the ton
But come up here in May
And, hey!, you're near as good as done.
For let the winter snow begin to
Melt a bit, and then:
Them billion bugs wake up and say,
"It's chow time again."

It's the Algonquin Breakdown!
Them views appeal to the artiste
But the beauty hides a beast!
The Algonquin Breakdown!
Where any normal lad
Is driven mad
By bugs and bogs and lice.
Welcome to Paradise!

DIXON is driven from the clearing by the flies. FRANCES settles back to wait.

Scene 20—You Could Use A Woman Like Me

Immediately following. THOMSON enters and crosses to his campsite, not seeing FRANCES. He sets up and starts to paint, but doesn't look happy at his results.

THOMSON: Damn! *(Tries again, but with no better results.)* Damn that grey!

FRANCES: I think it's rather good.

THOMSON turns to her.

FRANCES: Surprise!

She enjoys his amazement.

THOMSON: Frances!? How the hell did you get here?

FRANCES: A train. And then a very peculiar gentleman who insisted he was a guide.

THOMSON: Frances McGillvray in Algonquin Park. When was the last time you were north of Bloor Street?

FRANCES: The last time I was in that shack of yours in the city.

THOMSON: ...I remember.

FRANCES: Last month. It's good to see you. Of course, I thought I was going to see you last month.

THOMSON: I had to get out of the city.

FRANCES: Earlier every year. ...It wasn't a completely wasted trip, though. To your shack. Harris showed me those large canvases you're working on. The West Wind. The Jack Pine. I see you took my advice on that one sky.

THOMSON: Yes.

FRANCES: Those are the ones you're placing in the OSA this year?

THOMSON: I'm not showing this year.

FRANCES: Why not?

THOMSON: Because they aren't good enough.

FRANCES: ...They're beautiful. They'd sell in a second.

THOMSON: So have MacCallum sell them. I could use the money.

FRANCES: They deserve to be hung first. To be seen.

THOMSON: I'm not hanging them!

FRANCES: ...Well, isn't this going nicely so far? ...So this is where you run to every Spring. The flowers are beautiful. The wildflowers.

THOMSON: *(Of his board.)* Everywhere but here.

FRANCES: I'm trying to change the subject.

THOMSON: Oh.

FRANCES: ...Dammit, Tom, I'm fifty years old and I don't have the patience to beat around the bush. I like you, I like what you're trying to do—and you could use a woman like me. ...You're a good painter, Tom; I could help make you a better one.

THOMSON: It's art lessons you want to give me?

FRANCES: Those, too, if you want them. Frankly, the men I meet in Toronto these days you couldn't suck blood out of with a straw! Some even call themselves artists! You throw a glass of beer in their faces and they apologize to you. I'm sick to death of it! But you, Tom Thomson, have passion. And if you spend most of it on your painting so much the better. But just once I'd like the chance to mix my passion with some other primary colour—and just see what the hell happens.

THOMSON: ...I can't tie myself down.

FRANCES: So who brought rope?

THOMSON: I can't sit around some clapboard house and invite your parents for dinner on Sunday nights!

FRANCES: What, or who, are you talking about?

THOMSON: Time, Frances! Look!

He shows her some boards, shuffling them quickly.

I started in April to paint the Spring. Stop time on my boards. sixty of them. Paint the park every day April through June. The changes. The movement. The surprise. For weeks I couldn't do a damn thing. But now I can't keep up. I could paint sixty a week.

FRANCES: So do it. Time isn't the enemy, Tom.

THOMSON: It is! thirty-five years I wasted before I got here. And every year since I seem to fall farther behind. How do I catch up? How many bad paintings am I allowed before suddenly they start to seem good enough?

FRANCES: ...I don't know. But while you're waiting to be overwhelmed, while you're waiting for your paint and your passion to be thinned out until it disappears in the flood, you might just as well rage against it. ...I've always liked a little rage.

THOMSON: ...No more work today. We'll go for a walk. Pick some wildflowers.

FRANCES looks at the sky.

FRANCES: Just what I need in these shoes—a walk through the trees in the afternoon rain.

THOMSON looks up at the sky, suddenly invigorated.

THOMSON: Storm-front. Look at that grey!

And suddenly, forgetting all about FRANCES, he is back at work. He flips over his last board and starts in again on the other side, feverishly trying to capture the approaching storm. DIXON appears out of the trees.

DIXON: Need a guide back to the Mowat?

FRANCES smiles ruefully, looks at THOMSON, who no longer pays any attention to her, and starts to follow DIXON.

Part 4—Like A Seed In The Wind

Scene 21—The Gallery

Time and locations are beginning to overlap. Actions are blending, accelerating.

The Gallery Scene is split between an "Art Show" at the Mowat Lodge and other locations around the Park, including THOMSON's campsite and the Canoe Lake Cemetery.

Throughout the action on the Mowat Lodge Veranda, THOMSON remains at his campsite, sorting through sketches—studying them, discarding them, destroying them.

A waltz is playing. WINNIE waits impatiently on the Veranda, holding a small painting that she never looks at. ANNIE enters, carrying a painting.

ANNIE: Any sign of him yet?

WINNIE: No.

ANNIE: He'll be here.

SHANNON appears, but without a painting.

Shannon, did you put out those extra chairs?

SHANNON: That I did, darlin'.

ANNIE: And did you notice Tom arrive yet?

SHANNON: Now that I did not. ...Would you ever have guessed, Winnie, that a place run by the like of Shannon Fraser would ever end up an art gallery?

ANNIE: For one night anyway. And Shannon's been meaning to tell Tom how nice it was of him to make the offer. A free Tom Thomson painting for every Mowat Lodge guest—if that doesn't get people booking for next year, I don't know what will. I'll check inside again. Tell Winnie she mustn't worry, Shannon. *(Exits.)*

SHANNON: You mustn't worry, Winnie. It's my experience that Thomson always shows up eventually at the Mowat Lodge.

ANNIE's voice, and OTHERS, are heard singing "The Evening Sky". Eventually the song may overlap the sections of dialogue.

"The Evening Sky"

VOICES: There's a stir
In the stillness
Of the evening sky.
There's a song In the sunset
And there's you and I
Spinning gold In the moonlight
As we dance till dawn
On and on under evening sky.

SHANNON: ...Did you hear the latest from the war? We took Vimy Ridge.

WINNIE: Good news for a change.

SHANNON: Bletcher won't like it, of course. But first time they let the Canadians fight together and look what happens! ...I was in France, you know. Before I came here. You should see the hotels in France. Chandeliers, marble, starched cuffs. I always thought someday I'd own this really classy place. People—important people—would make a point to stay at Shannon Fraser's. I was even on my way up the ladder once but...well—I developed a reputation.

WINNIE: You and Annie do a wonderful job here.

SHANNON: Yes, well—my Annie. ...How does Thomson do that, Winnie? Change things? People. Ah, hell, I'm a rough man, I won't deny it. And never tried too hard to be anything else, truth be told. But my Annie...

VOICES: There's a glow
In the sunset
In the evening sky.
There's a wind,
And a whisper
And there's you and I
Dancing on in the sunset
As the colours pale
In the frail April evening sky.

ANNIE re-enters.

ANNIE: Anything yet?

WINNIE: No.

ANNIE: Still, it's going very well. You won't forget to thank Tom, will you, Shannon?

SHANNON: If he ever gets here, darlin', I'll be sure to thank him for all he's done for me.

SHANNON exits.

ANNIE: He's been so good all winter. Hasn't had a drink since Christmas. I think he's really trying hard, but—I don't know. He sees Tom, and how people react to his paintings. And now he sees me painting. I've seen him looking at my paintings when he doesn't know I'm watching him. It's like he's looking at something in himself somehow. At least, that's how I feel when I look at Tom's paintings.

ANNIE looks at the painting she's been carrying.

I think I like the skies in them the best. The evening skies.

VOICES: I feel the cool of the air,
Your wind-blown hair,
And your breath, like mist on my skin.
I see the high coloured kites
Of the Northern Lights,
And in your eyes
Are evening skies.

BLETCHER appears.

ANNIE: Hello, Martin. I see you chose a painting.

BLETCHER: Yes. I understood we were all expected to take one.

ANNIE: I should get back.

WINNIE: I'll come with you.

BLETCHER: Winnie…?

ANNIE exits.

BLETCHER: …I know you've never thought of me as—a suitor.

WINNIE: Martin, please…

BLETCHER: I need to say this. I know I'm not—I'm not at all like Thomson. But I've a good job. And a solid future…

WINNIE: Martin…

BLETCHER: And I love you. I'd be a good husband, Winnie—and father.

WINNIE: I can't marry you.

BLETCHER: I know you may feel you have other obligations.

But there are things you may not know. I was in Toronto. This winter.

WINNIE: And?

BLETCHER: And certain—information—came to my attention. About Thomson, and his relationships with certain —people.

WINNIE: What people?

FRANCES enters, carrying a painting. BLETCHER sees her and shuts up.

FRANCES: …I'm looking for Tom.

WINNIE: Join the vigil, Miss McGillvray.

FRANCES: Miss Trainor. *(To BLETCHER.)* And you are?

BLETCHER: Martin Bletcher.

FRANCES: Why do you look familiar, Mr. Bletcher? Have we met in Toronto?

BLETCHER: I'm from Buffalo.

FRANCES: …I've obviously interrupted something.

BLETCHER: No. …Excuse me.

BLETCHER exits.

FRANCES: I chose my allotted painting. *(Turns it over and reads the back.)* "Spring Ice", it says.

WINNIE: I was there the day he did that one. *(Points off.)* You can see the same island from here.

FRANCES: Different perspective.

WINNIE: Yes.

"Spring Ice (Teaser)"

VOICES: Spring Ice,
Winter melts away as
Spring Ice…

The Canoe Lake Burying Ground. WINNIE runs in. THOMSON comes in after her. Time shifts throughout this next section.

THOMSON: …What is this place?

WINNIE: It's what passes as the Canoe Lake Cemetery.

THOMSON: Charming place to be lured. *(Drawn to a gravestone.)* …Who's James Watson?

WINNIE: He was a mill-hand. Came here from Parry Sound and was killed his very first day on the job. Everyone up here knows the inscription by heart.

"Remember comrades when passing by
As you are now so once was I.
As I am now so you will be,
Prepare thyself to follow me."

THOMSON: I used to illustrate verses like that for a living.

WINNIE looks at a second grave.

WINNIE: This one is a little boy who died of diphtheria. He was eight.

THOMSON: …Both of them too young.

There is a subtle change as the scene moves back in time. THOMSON is looking around the area, more intently now.

The ice is starting to move on the water. The colours. Everything changing all the time.

WINNIE: No more painting today!

THOMSON: No.

WINNIE: Today's just for us. Hold me. …It's the beginning,

isn't it?

THOMSON holds her, looking off in the distance.

THOMSON: Yes.

Another shift.

WINNIE: ...I spoke to Annie about that art show idea for the Mowat. It's all set. It's nice of you to help them out, letting them give away your paintings.

THOMSON: It's either give them away or throw them away.

WINNIE: Look at me?

THOMSON: What am I looking for?

WINNIE: I don't know. As long as you know. Yes! Like that! Don't ever stop looking at me like that!

WINNIE is suddenly back at the Mowat. BLETCHER appears, watching her. WINNIE exits.

VOICES: There's a green
In the grey cloud
Of the midnight sky...
There's a wind,
And a wailing,
And there's you and I
Dancing on in the darkness
As the leaves swirl by...

SHANNON joins BLETCHER on the Veranda. BLETCHER now carries two paintings.

SHANNON: ...Bletcher. Got everything you need? Something to drink?

BLETCHER: *(Holds up a flask.)* Stopped by Dixon's on my way. You need one?

SHANNON: ...No. Promised Annie I wouldn't. Don't miss it, of course. I can take or leave a good drink. Doesn't matter to me. I don't need a drink. Water's fine. Tea.

Sarsaparilla, that's the ticket.

BLETCHER: I guess you saw the picture he did of you?

SHANNON: Of me?

BLETCHER shows SHANNON a board.

BLETCHER: In the sugar bush. You ask me, he's painted you pretty much the colour of dried blood.

SHANNON: Any there of Annie?

BLETCHER: I didn't see one. But some may not be for us to see.

SHANNON: And I hear talk Thomson and Winnie plan to be married.

BLETCHER slowly moves from his scene with SHANNON to his scene with THOMSON, then eventually sharply back again. BLETCHER looks at his other painting.

BLETCHER: ...I went out to the dam. Where he camps. Told him I'd been in Toronto this winter. That I'd watched him.

THOMSON: The investigator investigates.

BLETCHER: I told him I'd seen him with that Miss McGillvray. And with the wife of one of his own painter friends.

BLETCHER is now at the dam, confronting THOMSON directly.

...In my line of work I see men like you all the time. Poor boring businessmen pay me good money to find out where their poor bored wives go in the afternoon. Well, they go to men like you.

THOMSON: Leave it alone, Bletcher.

BLETCHER: It's not only you who wants things. So does everyone else in this park. But what comes so easily to you doesn't come so easily to the rest of us. You take what she gives you but you don't appreciate it. Like you dismiss your own paintings. A man should be proud of what he does. And who he loves.

THOMSON: Winnie doesn't love you, Bletcher.

BLETCHER: She could. If it weren't for you!

THOMSON: Nothing comes easily, Bletcher. You want something, you hack through the brush and go get it.

BLETCHER: I want you out of this park, Thomson. I want you the hell out of this park!

BLETCHER snaps his board in two. WINNIE, ANNIE and FRANCES enter, separated from SHANNON and BLETCHER.

ANNIE: Shannon, people are starting to leave. I need you to come be the perfect host.

WINNIE: I should be going, too.

FRANCES: You still haven't shown us which piece you chose, Miss Trainor.

WINNIE looks at the painting she's been holding the entire scene.

WINNIE: I look at this, and I see what's possible. I see what Tom can do with the right subject.

WINNIE shows FRANCES her painting.

FRANCES: Surely that's not one of Tom's.

ANNIE looks at WINNIE's painting.

ANNIE: No. That's one of mine.

SHANNON looks again at his painting.

SHANNON: God, I need a drink.

The Veranda of the Mowat Lodge disappears.

Scene 22—Painter Goes Mad

THOMSON's campsite. MacCALLUM appears with THOMSON. MacCALLUM has a book. He reads the cover page.

MacCALLUM: "I must do my own work and live my own way because I am responsible for both."

THOMSON: Rudyard Kipling.

MacCALLUM: Yes. "The Light That Failed". Wonderful name "Rudyard". Who do you know these days would name their son "Rudyard"?

THOMSON: You still could, Doctor.

MacCALLUM: I'd be afraid of having a son lest he turn out like you—and call me "Doctor" my entire life. Did you read the book, or just design that beautifully engraved plate of the noble quote?

THOMSON: I read the book.

MacCALLUM: Then you remember what happened. Painter creates exquisite painting, painter goes blind. Painter then becomes obsessed, painter's painting destroyed, painter goes mad, dies horrible tragic death. True, it's a 19th century novel. But there is a moral here, Tom. Do your work. Get paid for your work. Go home to your wife and children. One child of whom should be named Rudyard.

THOMSON: ...I was working this morning—I'd done three or four boards and I wanted to move on. So I left what I'd finished on the trail to dry and I went up to the point and I did a couple more. I come back down the trail to pick up the first ones. And I hear something. Scratching. So I come to where I'd left my boards and what do I see? A lynx. Grey. The kind of grey I can never goddam get. And this lynx is scratching the hell out of my boards. Paint all over its paws but it keeps scratching. Suddenly it stops and looks at me. Just sort of looks at me, then looks at these paintings it's been clawing. It felt like about a month we stood there. Finally it sort of sneezes and disappears into the trees. Of course the boards are ruined. Now I think—this lynx has lived here all its life—it knows these trees a helluva lot better than I ever will. Like a true critic it told me in no uncertain terms just what the hell it thought of my painting. In fact that goddamn *grey* lynx is telling me what I been telling myself for years.

MacCALLUM: Perhaps, my friend, he thought it was a tree.

THOMSON: You missed my Art Show at the Mowat.

MacCALLUM: As I understand it, so did you. Besides, an Art Show where paintings are given away is too painful a place for an agent. But it's not your paintings I'm concerned about at the moment, it's you.

THOMSON: ...What's the difference?

MacCALLUM disappears as WINNIE appears.

WINNIE: ...We missed you.

THOMSON: At Annie's, yes. I meant to be there.

WINNIE: It's not important. Did you write them in Bella Lake yet?

THOMSON: No, not yet.

WINNIE: Do you want me to do it?

THOMSON: ...Do what?

WINNIE: Write them in Bella Lake!

THOMSON: No, I'll do it.

WINNIE: Late summer's their busy time, we need reservations....

THOMSON: I know. I'll do it.

WINNIE: ...I need you to write them in Bella Lake.

WINNIE disappears; and FRANCES is there.

FRANCES: I'm taking today's train back, Tom. ...My offer, if you remember it, still stands.

THOMSON hands her a painted vase.

What's this?

THOMSON: I've been painting plates for Winnie. Dinner plates. Ashtrays. Vases. ...It's a nice change to paint something people might actually have a use for.

FRANCES gives THOMSON back the vase.

FRANCES: ...You're too good not to show in the OSA, Tom.

THOMSON hands her the vase again, more tenderly.

THOMSON: Put flowers in it. Hang it in the OSA. ...Thanks for your help with that sky.

FRANCES disappears as WINNIE, ANNIE and SHANNON appear. ANNIE now has the vase.

WINNIE: Annie has the vase you painted for Frances. And she doesn't understand how it could have been left behind.

SHANNON: My Annie.

WINNIE: She's going to send it down to her in the city, she said, as soon as she can.

THOMSON: It was just a vase.

WINNIE: She showed me how pretty it looks in the light.

SHANNON: How does he do that, Winnie?

THOMSON: I figured vase painting was one thing I could probably keep under control.

SHANNON: Change things. People.

BLETCHER appears.

BLETCHER: I'm not afraid of you!

WINNIE: Nothing's under control!

BLETCHER: Are you and Winnie getting married? Is it true you've booked a honeymoon at Bella Lake?

WINNIE: I thought you wanted to make these plans!

THOMSON: I do.

SHANNON: I bested your strong hand!

MacCALLUM appears.

MacCALLUM: I wonder how I shall ultimately feel about this Park, Tom…

FRANCES appears.

FRANCES: Time isn't the enemy.

BLETCHER: Answer me!

FRANCES: Just rage against it.

WINNIE: Hold me.

MacCALLUM: …if it proves to have cured me, but destroyed you.

WINNIE reacts as if THOMSON has put his arms around her, though he stands isolated from all of them.

BLETCHER: A man should be proud of what he does. And who he loves.

WINNIE: Tighter.

WINNIE reacts as if THOMSON has hugged her more tightly.

Throughout this sequence, ANNIE has been in the process of placing the vase on the shelf, staring at it oddly. Suddenly, however, there is the crash of the breaking vase. ANNIE reacts as the vase hits the floor. The music becomes angry and powerful.

ANNIE: Tom, I'm sorry.

THOMSON: Annie!

ANNIE: It was an accident, I swear.

THOMSON: You did it on purpose!

WINNIE: Look at me?

SHANNON: God, I need a drink!

ANNIE: No, I swear —it just slipped though my fingers.

MacCALLUM: Painter goes mad.

ANNIE: It was just a vase!

DIXON: Kindling.

BLETCHER: I want you out of this park!

WINNIE: Please don't ever stop looking at me like that.

FRANCES: You're too damn good not to show in the OSA, Tom!

SHANNON: Tommy.

BLETCHER: Thomson!

WINNIE: Tom?!?!

"Colours In The Storm"

THOMSON: The Colours in the Storm
Burn like the sun.
The Colours in the Storm
Roar like thunder.
Sparks of light among the dark,
Vulture and lark,
Together form
The Colours in the Storm.

The fevers in the wind
Rumble and purr.
The blood-red and the grey
Rage like hurricane. In the silence and the din,
Outside and in,
Form
The Colours in the Storm.

COMPANY: I
And the colours in the sky
Are churning,
Changing.
Energized,
Paralyzed,
Colour-blind.

The Colours in the Storm
Sing like a swan,
You catch them here in paint,
Then they're gone again.
Through the stillness and the flight,
The darkness and light
Fly (Fly, Fly, Fly)
The Colours in the Storm
And I!

THOMSON collapses to his knees.

Part Five—Take Me With You

Scene 23—Something In The Water Off Shore

ROBINSON consults his diary.

ROBINSON: On Sunday July 8th, 1917, Tom starts off with his fishing equipment, and a lunch packed for him by Shannon Fraser.

DIXON: He'd told me that morning he was going over to Gill Lake to catch as large a trout as he could, and then tell Mark Robinson that it was the Baron. But I was at Gill Lake the whole day, settin'… *(Stops, looks at ROBINSON.)* …settin' on a rock. I never saw Tom that whole day.

ROBINSON: …We none of us ever saw Tom alive again. Monday the 9th, Martin Bletcher…

DIXON: I'd like to ask *him* a few questions, I would.

ROBINSON: …reports having seen Thomson's canoe overturned the day before.

DIXON: And did nothin' about it! Towed Tom's canoe to his own boathouse, then waited a whole day to report it!

ROBINSON: Upon examination of the canoe, none of Tom's equipment is found…

DIXON: Except the portaging paddle.

ROBINSON: …except the portaging paddle.

DIXON: Which wasn't even knotted down proper. Tom would've never knotted it like that.

ROBINSON: When no word is heard from Tom by Wednesday, an official search is finally begun.

DIXON: And what about his working paddle? Never found. Paddles float, you know. Paddles don't just sink to the bottom of a lake like a shotgun. And then the canoe disappears!

ROBINSON: The search continues through the following Sunday, but there's no trace. Then Monday the 16th, a Dr. George Howland, vacationing on an island in Canoe Lake, notices something in the water off shore. He calls to a passing canoeist…

DIXON: That was me.

ROBINSON: …to investigate.

DIXON: And it was then we found Tom's body.

Cross-fade to next scene.

Scene 24—Ain't That Why You Should Come?

THOMSON's campsite. He is suddenly aware of WILD MARY.

THOMSON: …It's you.

WILD MARY: Whoever I am.

THOMSON: What is it you want?

WILD MARY: Do I get a picture yet?

THOMSON offers a sketch. She looks at it impassively.

Not so good, is it?

She hands back the sketch and moves closer to the trees.

Come.

She starts to leave, expecting him to follow.

THOMSON: …No.

WILD MARY: You afraid?

THOMSON: I don't know anything about you.

WILD MARY: Ain't that why you should come?

THOMSON: …Where then? To see what?

WILD MARY: Through the shadows. Through the pine. Into the heart.

She touches him again. He again reacts away.

Up to you.

This time she moves to the edge of the shadows. She holds out her hand but he stays where he is. She drops her hand, suddenly stretches to her full height, preening, keening like a mating animal, then disappears. THOMSON runs to the spot, but can no longer see her.

THOMSON: No, wait! Wait, I'll come!

THOMSON tries to follow her, but she is gone. He gets confused in the trees as he tries to find her. He is suddenly in his canoe, paddling. ROBINSON joins him.

Scene 25—Just A Little Farther

A distant lake. THOMSON and ROBINSON paddling a canoe. THOMSON paddles slowly and steadily throughout this scene. They paddle silently awhile—listening, watching, absorbing. ROBINSON gets impatient and stops paddling.

ROBINSON: We gonna stop and fish or what?

THOMSON silently keeps paddling.

Christmas, Tom—even *your* arms have to be tired by now.

THOMSON: Just up around the next point.

ROBINSON: *(Looking around.)* Where in blazes are we anyway? I thought I knew every inch of this park. You even know where in blazes we are?

No answer from THOMSON. The two of them paddle on again. ROBINSON watches the point go by.

OK, so we passed the point. All I see is more o' the same. Can we fish now?

THOMSON: Just a little farther.

ROBINSON: You're possessed. Jiggered if I know how you expect to find the Baron way in blazes out here anyway.

THOMSON: I'll find him.

ROBINSON: We've portaged three times. He's a trout not a confounded voyageur! *(Pause.)* Can we fish, please?!

THOMSON: Mark? Relax. When was the last time you saw a morning like this? Drink it in, my friend, while the light lasts.

ROBINSON: The best meal money can buy at Mowat Lodge says you can't catch the Baron before the summer's out.

THOMSON: You're betting a meal at Mowat Lodge? Who has to eat it—the winner or the loser?

ROBINSON: We got a bet or don't we?

THOMSON: Loser has Shannon fly in the best Alberta beef-steak ever tumbled off the rib. You can order mine rare.

ROBINSON: Might as well settle for steak, we're sure never gonna eat trout... So it's a wager? Before the summer's out?

THOMSON: Before the colour hits the maple.

ROBINSON: Done! Easiest steak I'll ever win! Now—before the colour hits the maple, can we fish please?!

THOMSON: Just around the next turn in the water.

ROBINSON: Possessed! The man's blessed possessed!

THOMSON continues his steady paddling and finally ROBINSON joins him. They head for the next turn in the water.

Scene 26—The West Wind

FRANCES appears, watching THOMSON paint.

"The West Wind"

FRANCES: There's a solitary pine,
Like a harp against the sky,
Waiting for the wind's inspiration.
Bending just above the shoreline,
Ragged to the eye,
Quivering in still anticipation.

WILD MARY appears, moving in towards THOMSON.

WOMEN: And then the wind begins to stir,
And the water to purr,
And like the tuning of old instruments
The shore and lake and sky become alive.

THOMSON becomes aware of WILD MARY. Throughout the rest of the song, WILD MARY tries to lead THOMSON into a greater awareness of himself and the overpowering elements of the park. She challenges him, taunts him, inspires him. He struggles to "see" everything She tries to show him.

COMPANY: And the jack pine dances,
And the jack pine sings,
As the clouds from the west
Soar on painted wings

And though the wind makes the pine-boughs
ache,
Those branches refuse to break.

And the jack pine scuttles,
As the west wind bites,
As the waves on the lake
Peak in greys and whites.
And though it's dizzied by the raging squall,
The jack pine refuses to fall.

There's a stubborn northern pine
With its roots dug into stone
Daring any storm to defy it.
In the windy cloud-whipped sunshine,
Steadfast and alone,
Longing for the storm to rage riot.
Because the harder that wind blows,
The stronger that tree grows.
And as the gale blows blue to purple-gray
And greens and reds the jack pine comes alive.

THOMSON's experience with WILD MARY, as with the colours and secrets of the park, continues to intensify.

COMPANY: And the jack pine dances,
And the jack pine sings,
As the song goes deep
Into its jack pine rings.
And though the west wind may bend it back,
It will not be made to crack.
Yes, the jack pine revels In the west wind gale,
For that wind blows heavy
But to avail,
For the harder it blows,
And the higher it throws its spray…

THOMSON seems finally to see what it is he's been looking for. He is elated, inspired.

The jack pine grows stronger,
And dances away!

THOMSON revels in the park and the possibilities in his painting. But just as he seems finally to be satisfied, that satisfaction seems suddenly to slip away. He doesn't know what to try next.

Scene 27—Death By Drowning

ROBINSON and DIXON step forward again to address the audience.

ROBINSON: Late morning, July 16th. When it's clear who it is has been found, Dr. Howland examines the body immediately. There was fishing line wrapped sixteen or seventeen times around one ankle, no water in the lungs, evidence of bleeding from one ear, and a four inch bruise across the left temple.

DIXON: As if struck by the edge of a paddle.

ROBINSON: It was a bruise. Coulda happened a hundred ways.

DIXON: Sure. And a canoe and paddle just disappear without a trace.

ROBINSON: He concludes death by drowning.

DIXON: And no water in the lungs.

ROBINSON: When the coroner is delayed, the Park Superintendent authorizes the body to be buried in the small Canoe Lake cemetery. Martin Bletcher Sr. reads the service. Winnie Trainor leaves the same night for Huntsville.

DIXON and ROBINSON exit.

Scene 28—The Wind In Your Hair

Outside the Trainor Cottage, Saturday, July 7th. Night. THOMSON is weeding the garden. WINNIE enters, looking for him.

WINNIE: …Tom? *(No response.)* Is that you? …What are you doing?

THOMSON: Working on the garden.

WINNIE: It's pitch black out here!

THOMSON: There's enough light. Look at all the stars.

WINNIE: Come inside.

THOMSON: Remember that first Spring? The night I met your parents? You made me help you with the garden.

WINNIE: I remember.

THOMSON: I look forward to this. It takes my mind off things.

WINNIE: We did the garden two months ago. It's July, Tom.

THOMSON: And the day we shot those rapids. …Remember?

WINNIE: …I remember.

THOMSON: *(Admiring his work.)* That looks better. …I think.

WINNIE: …I'm going back inside.

THOMSON: I used to know when I made you angry. I always loved how you never let me get away with anything.

WINNIE: I'm not angry.

THOMSON: You want to make plans; I haven't been very helpful. …When I first saw you, the wind had caught your hair, and it looked so wild!

WINNIE: What the wind does with my hair is not me!

THOMSON: It is! …I've been thinking of going to the Rockies.

Here in the Park—maybe I've been painting the same things for too long—but it's like I can't take the next step—turn the next bend. I haven't painted for weeks. I thought maybe somewhere else…

WINNIE: No one's stopping you. But are you going to the Rockies? Or running away from here?

THOMSON: I want to be wherever I have to be.

WINNIE: You don't have to be somewhere else! Look what you've done here!

THOMSON: What I've done isn't the point! What I'm capable of is the point! Winnie…it's like when the light hits the water just so, and you see this—amazing colour! It's there then it's gone. A fraction of a second. You get it down on a board, and there it is! But then someone says it doesn't look right—no, you couldn't possibly have seen *that* colour. You know it existed but you can't prove it to anyone else! And then you begin to doubt. Maybe what you thought you saw was never really there. Maybe you still haven't got it right! Suddenly, you have to go on faith. And faith is so hard!

WINNIE: Faith in what? That you're going to be a great painter?

THOMSON: Great painter…! I'm no different than you or Dixon or Annie…

WINNIE: You are not like the rest of us, Tom! Ordinary people don't weed gardens in the middle of the night!

THOMSON: There's no such thing as an "ordinary" person.

WINNIE: Of course there is. I'm one of them.

THOMSON: No.

WINNIE: Ordinary, everyday people who grow up! Who face facts—limitations!

THOMSON: I did that for thirty-five years. No more!

WINNIE: Alright! But I'm not like you! I have to know what to expect, Tom. Now. Tonight!

THOMSON: Come with me!

WINNIE: ...What?

THOMSON: Now. Tonight! To the Rockies. To France!

WINNIE: No! Stop it!

THOMSON: To hell with our plans! Things change too fast! You have to catch them. Colour them. Before they're gone. We can do that! Winnie, you can do that! It takes courage, sure. Yes, it's a risk. But we only get so many chances and I nearly missed mine. Thirty-five years old and what was I?! The man I was before I got here you wouldn't have wanted.

WINNIE: Stop.

THOMSON: *(Barreling right along.)* I wouldn't let you settle for a man like I was before I found all this —before I finally faced what it is in me that needs to do this! Face that in yourself, Winnie!

WINNIE: I said, stop! You think you're the only one with courage? Who's willing to take risks? What are you in my life if not a risk—one that up until this very moment I've been willing to take. Who's the one here with courage, Tom; and who's the one running away? I think you're a fake! I think that for all your strength, and your passion, and your genius if that's what it is, I think you're the one who's afraid—afraid to really look at yourself, and us—and see what's wonderful here and now. The thought of living the rest of my life with you is wonderful, and exciting, and so frightening. But if all you can see when you look at us is what's frightening, then you're the coward, Tom, not me. ...I'm not one of those jack pines you paint. Those damn pines that never really look like you paint them to look. But I love you. Please. Come inside.

THOMSON: ...We'll leave tonight.

WINNIE pulls away from him.

...I need you, Winnie. But I need you with the wind in your hair.

WINNIE exits. THOMSON is alone.

Scene 29—She Looks Real, The Moon's Just Right

THOMSON is outside DIXON's shack. DIXON enters from inside, several sheets to the wind.

DIXON: ...Whozat? Thomson, that you? You here for hooch?

THOMSON: I'm here to get out of the rain.

DIXON: What?

THOMSON: You told me once, if it was raining, I should come to your shack.

DIXON: It ain't raining.

THOMSON: I found that pine.

DIXON: So?

THOMSON: ...You know Wild Mary? You know where I can find her?

DIXON: ...Sure.

THOMSON: I have to talk to her.

DIXON: Now that's gonna be harder.

THOMSON: I have to.

DIXON: The woman's dead, Thomson. Been dead fifteen years.

THOMSON: No. I've seen her.

DIXON: I buried her myself. ...I come out here for something.

THOMSON: No. She was real.

DIXON: She looks real, the moon's just right. I saw her once, standing right on the spot I buried her. When I went to hold her, she was gone.

SHANNON: *(Offstage.)* Dixon...!

DIXON: ...You better go, too. Fraser's inside. And Bletcher. The way they're talking, best you stay away from them tonight. Go to Winnie's. Or the Lodge. How did you manage to get so many people mad at you all at the same time?

THOMSON: I love her, you know. I do.

DIXON starts rummaging through his woodpile for something and pulls out a board or two.

Hey, what's that?

DIXON: Kindling.

THOMSON: These are old boards of mine—where'd you get all these?!

DIXON: I didn't steal nuthin'. Some you gave me. And some I found on the trail where you'd thrown 'em.

THOMSON: Look at them! Is it any wonder I tossed them?

DIXON: Ever since that one of my shack sold for four hundred I been collectin' these things for my old age.

DIXON has found some hooch and takes a swig.

Let's go. ...Gotta find Wild Mary.

DIXON sways off, but THOMSON is too caught up in his boards. SHANNON enters from the shack. He too has been drinking.

SHANNON: Dixon, what's keeping that hooch? ...Well—if it ain't the great Tom Thomson. Come by for an arm-wrestle, have ya?

THOMSON continues examining the boards.

Or is it paintin' lessons tonight? Is my Annie here, too, then—to learn to paint the moon!? I miss her, ya know that, Thomson? My Annie? The Annie who used to think I was somethin'—who needed Shannon Fraser to make *her* feel like somethin'. Could ya change me, too, Thomson, like ya done my Annie, by givin' me paintin' lessons?!

BLETCHER enters.

BLETCHER: ...What's he doing here? No women here. ...We've been talking about you, Thomson. I've been a little worried how Fraser hasn't been quite himself lately. *(Pours FRASER a drink.)* He's more himself tonight. I've been telling him the kind of thing you're up to every winter in the city. The kind of thing you're probably up to here in the park.

THOMSON is still paying little attention.

Are you listening to me?! The kind of man you are, Thomson, doesn't deserve a woman like Winnie! And I am not going to stand by any longer watching you destroy things!

SHANNON: Forget it, Martin, it ain't worth the effort.

BLETCHER: Like it ain't worth the effort to keep the man away from your own wife?!

SHANNON: I can take care of my own wife! Do I look like I ain't noticed how he's been makin' my Annie think she deserves better than Shannon Fraser?!

BLETCHER: So, what are you going to do about it?

SHANNON: I'll do what I have to, if it's any business of yours,

Bletcher!

BLETCHER: Isn't that what you think, Thomson? That Annie deserves a damn sight better than Shannon Fraser?

THOMSON: What I think, Bletcher, is that Winnie deserves a helluva lot better than you.

BLETCHER: It seems he's a better man than both of us, Fraser.

SHANNON: Well, then maybe it's time he finally proved it. You want my wife, Thomson, challenge me to a duel! Drown me in my sleep and the two of you can go off together to paint the moon!

THOMSON: I don't want to fight you, Shannon.

SHANNON: Ain't that just the picture of the man?! Backing away from a challenge. Too much of an "Artist" to fight! Takes guts to fight for somethin' with your "good hand", Thomson. 'Cause then you got no excuses if you lose!

SHANNON pushes THOMSON, THOMSON reacts back. SHANNON pushes THOMSON again. THOMSON staggers away, recovers, but keeps his back to SHANNON. SHANNON pulls THOMSON towards him again.

Turn around and fight, goddamn it!

With a vicious blow SHANNON knocks the wind out of THOMSON. As THOMSON tries to recover, SHANNON hits him again. THOMSON is knocked to the ground where he hits his head and lies dead still. SHANNON can't react—the explosion of his anger has left him momentarily disoriented. He looks at THOMSON in horror.

...Oh, god! I've killed him! Dammit, Bletcher, he's dead!

BLETCHER: He's not dead.

SHANNON: Oh, god!

BLETCHER: It's just a cut. Get a rag—a bandage. Don't just stand there!

SHANNON: Look at the blood! He hit his head on the trap and... Oh, my god!

BLETCHER: Keep your voice down.

SHANNON, frightened and confused, runs away from the cabin into the trees.

Shannon! Shannon, get back here!

BLETCHER looks at THOMSON, then exits after SHANNON.

WILD MARY appears. She has been watching. She goes to the unmoving THOMSON and touches his forehead. He groans and begins to stir, then rouses himself groggily, wincing from the pain in his forehead. Finding himself among DIXON's collection of his "boards", his anger and frustration peak, and he starts destroying the boards, ripping them apart and tossing them aside.

Only after the worst of his fury is spent does he become aware of WILD MARY, who has taken one board from the chaos and looked at it.

WILD MARY: I'll take this one.

WILD MARY shows THOMSON the board. He eyes it oddly, trying to focus on it as clearly as he can.

THOMSON: ...Oh, god. ...Oh, god. Look at that grey! I got the damn grey!

WILD MARY leads THOMSON into shadow.

Scene 30—I Still Believe Tom's Body Is Buried Right Here

ROBINSON: Late on the night of Tuesday July 17th, the coroner finally arrives in the Park and an inquest is held in the home of Martin Bletcher.

DIXON: Of all places.

ROBINSON: Without seeing the body, the coroner takes evidence, mainly from Dr Howland, and concludes death by drowning. No one else has much to say.

DIXON: I had plenty to say, only I weren't invited.

ROBINSON: Next night, an undertaker from Huntsville arrives to exhume Tom's body and return it to the family cemetery near Owen Sound. This happens without my knowledge. And according to Shannon Fraser, who helps the undertaker carry the coffin to the train, the coffin shipped to Owen Sound isn't heavy enough to contain a body.

DIXON: Don't none of it make no sense.

ROBINSON: His relatives in Leith insist Tom's body is in the casket when it is buried in the family churchyard.

DIXON: But Shannon Fraser swears…

ROBINSON: *(Interrupting.)* And the family makes it clear they want nothing further to do with solving any "mysteries" about the whereabouts of Tom's body. Officially, it is death by drowning, and Tom's body is reinterred in Leith, Ontario.

DIXON: He was our friend. It shoulda none of it ever happened. *(Exits.)*

ROBINSON: I've never been sure why I couldn't speak up that night. Maybe it was where the inquest was held—maybe it was who else was in the room. But I said it later and I'll state right here that I don't believe Tom Thomson died an accidental death from drowning that afternoon of July 8th. *(He starts to leave, but stops again.)* And God forgive me if I'm wrong, but I still believe Tom's body is buried right here.

He places a flower on the grave. Then exits.

Scene 31 —Because Of What He Saw In Me

The Canoe Lake Cemetery, 1921. WINNIE is gathering flowers that have been scattered on THOMSON's grave. FRANCES appears behind her. THOMSON watches them.

FRANCES: Hello... You may not remember me. Frances McGillvray. We met a few years ago.

WINNIE: The year Tom died. The vase. I remember.

FRANCES: I thought they moved the body.

WINNIE: Kids from the summer camps come and leave flowers. I guess they think it's respectful.

FRANCES: You keep it well tended.

Again a silence for a few moments.

It must have been hard for you. I understand you were to be married.

WINNIE: Did Tom tell you that?

FRANCES: No.

WINNIE: Then we're discussing a rumour, aren't we? And I don't discuss rumours.

FRANCES: I'm sorry.

WINNIE: ...You're from the city. You were one of Tom's artist friends.

FRANCES: Yes.

WINNIE: So many people were interested in him because he was an artist. A good artist, I guess.

FRANCES: Yes.

THOMSON moves through them, sensed but unseen.

THOMSON: If I were to paint Winnie Trainor—if you were water, or wildflowers or sky—what colours would I use? No grey. Yellows, blues, and today—reds.

FRANCES: Miss Trainor…? …I'm sorry, I shouldn't have intruded. I'm not usually sentimental about this kind of thing. But it's eerie. Everywhere you look here you see one of his paintings. Look out there. It's as if…

THOMSON: *(To FRANCES.)* No more work today. We'll go for a walk. Pick some wildflowers.

WINNIE: …I'll let you have a few minutes alone.

FRANCES: No, please. …I feel him, too.

WINNIE: Did he talk to you? About painting? Is that why you loved him? Because of what he said about his painting? How he *felt* about it?

FRANCES: No.

THOMSON: Look at the light on the water. It looks like one colour—but it's dozens of colours. Can you see them?

FRANCES: It was never what he *said* about things that mattered. It was what he saw.

WINNIE: And I tried to see that. I tried so hard.

THOMSON: The colour of everything changes all the time.

FRANCES: Until Tom came back from this park for the first time, I'd forgotten how some people can look at you—as if they can see into the very part of you you've tried so hard to keep hidden. It was wonderful, and awful...

WINNIE: ...and frightening.

THOMSON: Fly with me to the Rockies, Winnie Trainor. Now. Tonight!

FRANCES: So many people are going to be moved by what he did—are going to love him because of what he saw in these trees, and this water and that sky. ...Why did you love him?

WINNIE: ...Because of what he saw in me.

"Spring Ice"

Spring Ice
Winter melts away as
Spring Ice
What was frozen solid
Trembles In the sunlight
And moves.

FRANCES: Spring Ice
I was turned one day to
Spring Ice
What was frozen in me
Trembled
His was the one light
That moved me.

BOTH: I could feel my eyes
Begin to glisten and shine
I could feel his eyes
Reach into mine.
I could feel my hair
Sweep up like mist in the sky
And fly.

Spring Ice
Winter melts away

As Spring Ice
And now what flows in me
Is trembling
For suddenly look! Spring is gone
And summer moves me on.

FRANCES and WINNIE exit.

Scene 32—It's Like Shooting Rapids

THOMSON: It's like shooting rapids. You're never sure if it's you in control, or the river. I dumped once in white water; and there we were, ass over tea-kettle bulleting down this river—me, the canoe, my kit, and all the boards I'd done over the last week. It was a near thing, but I made it. Eventually I bailed the canoe, my clothes dried and the campfire burned the water off the bacon. But those boards? I'd done one the same day of that river—tried to get the roar in paint, the colour of the under-pull, the power. When I'd finished with that board, it sang. It threatened. ...And it didn't last the day. ...It's funny—people say oil and water don't mix—well, here what had once been water in oil was now more water than oil and all the colours running like rivers themselves and the whole damn mess no use to anybody. And it kinda made me think of those old fields that get reclaimed over the years by the forests they'd once been cleared from. Ashes to ashes, dust to dust, and water in oil to water. ...But I'm damned if I didn't scrape that board down and start in on it again the next day. And the first picture I did was of that white water.

"Northern River (Reprise)"

WILD MARY: Standing in the shadows,

THOMSON: *(Holds up his board.)* Look.

WILD MARY: Looking towards the light

THOMSON: Look at that!

WILD MARY: Wondering where the river goes.

WINNIE: That's what makes it an adventure.

WILD MARY: Hovering on the water

THOMSON: I finally got all of this!

WILD MARY: Trees and sky unite

THOMSON: All of this!

WILD MARY: Flowing where the river flows.

DIXON: He was our friend. It shoulda none of it ever happened.

COMPANY: Northern River

THOMSON: *(Seeing something else.)* Oh, no.

COMPANY: Can we ever know

THOMSON: Oh, damn.

COMPANY: Where these Northern Rivers

THOMSON: It's changing again!

COMPANY: Go?

FRANCES: You might as well rage against it.

COMPANY: Pine wood arms to hold me
Dark and cool and still
I'm frightened how the river burns.

LAWREN HARRIS: And I am certain that what we saw that night was the spirit of Tom Thomson.

MacCALLUM: *(Overlapping.)* …Tom Thomson. Painter.

COMPANY: Wind sweeps up behind me
Rustling down the hill
Drawn to where the river turns.

ROBINSON: And God forgive me if I'm wrong, but I still believe
Tom's body is buried right here.
My face would ripple in the water

COMPANY: Northern River
Can we learn to read
Where these Northern Rivers
Lead?

WILD MARY: Through the shadows. Through the pine. Into the heart.

THOMSON: Were I to step out of the trees
And dare the river
Open to the skies

COMPANY: And I would float
Like a seed in the wind
The colours on the river
The colours in my eyes.

Northern River
Dare we ever know
Where these Northern Rivers
Go?
Changing greys and blue
Northern River
Take me with you!

The End.